MORAL PHILOSOPHY

A. R. C. DUNCAN, PROFESSOR OF PHILOSOPHY,
QUEEN'S UNIVERSITY
SIX RADIO LECTURES BROADCAST ON CBC
UNIVERSITY OF THE AIR

CANADIAN BROADCASTING CORPORATION, TORONTO

0-88794-050-1

Printed in Canada for

CBC PUBLICATIONS

Box 500, Terminal A, Toronto 116

by T. H. Best Printing Company Limited

This book contains the text of six half-hour radio lectures first broadcast on CBC University of the Air early in 1965. The series was arranged by Phyllis Webb and produced by Lynn Higgins, CBC Department of Public Affairs.

Alastair Robert Campbell Duncan was born in Scotland in 1915. He was educated at George Watson's Boys' College and the University of Edinburgh, where he graduated M.A. with First-Class Honours in Philosophy in 1936. A year as German Exchange Student at the University of Marburg was followed by two years teaching: first as assistant lecturer at Edinburgh; then as lecturer at University College, the University of London. After war-time service as Regimental Officer in the Royal Artillery and as General Staff Officer, Grade III, with Military Intelligence in North Africa, Italy, and the War Office, he returned to Edinburgh University in 1945 as lecturer and director of studies. In 1949, he was appointed John and Ella Charlton Professor of Philosophy and Head of the Department at Queen's University, where he was Dean of the Faculty of Arts and Sciences from 1959 to 1964. Professor Duncan's publications include *Practical Reason and Morality* (1957), articles on philosophy and education, and a translation, H.-J. de Vleeschauwer's *The Development of Kantian Thought* (1962). He is a member of the Mind Association, the Aristotelian Society, and the Royal Institute of Philosophy.

CONTENTS

MORAL PHILOSOPHY

MORAL PHILOSOPHY

1

Since the fifth century B.C. moral philosophy has attracted the energies of nearly all the outstanding philosophers in the Western tradition. None of them has underestimated the difficulty or the importance of this branch of philosophy. Plato put the problem very succinctly when he observed that "it is no light matter to discuss the course we must follow if we are to live our lives to the best advantage". No light matter indeed, but in the twentieth century the task of the moral philosopher has been greatly complicated by a number of factors that produce considerable confusion concerning the nature of that task and his hopes of achieving it. If we do not begin by attempting to remove some of the causes of this confusion, there is a serious danger that our whole discussion will be shipwrecked on the jagged rocks of misunderstanding.

To begin with, it is commonplace to say that Western civilization is now well and truly launched into the age of science. This has already affected general education. Everyone has some idea of what science is and everyone knows how science has made possible the mechanical devices that improve our material standard of living. However, there is no such widespread understanding of philosophy, what philosophy is or what it can hope to achieve. The philosopher is required to justify himself almost before he is given a hearing. Some people have urged that in an age of science philosophy is simply outmoded or that its only hope of salvation lies in its becoming scientific. This means that the moral philosopher, who is not trying to do the sort of thing that the scientist does so well, must not only explain what moral philosophy is, but what philosophy itself is.

Secondly, moral philosophy is concerned with morality, and about the nature of morality there is today so much confusion and misunderstanding that it is difficult to find some common ground from which discussion can profitably begin. In an article that appeared recently in a large Canadian daily newspaper, the writer surveys at some length the current state of public morality and gloomily asserts that "it does not seem extreme to wonder whether ethics are becoming obsolete". The sentence that I have just quoted is evidence of the type of confusion I have in mind. The standards of ethics or morality may deteriorate in a society, as the writer also suggests, but morality itself, which belongs to the very stuff of human life, is not the kind of thing that can become obsolete. This writer was so perturbed by current moral practice that he conducted a poll of twenty persons here in Toronto. He explained that they became quite candid in answering his questions when they were assured that they would not be identified. The results of this informal poll are interesting and I should like to quote verbatim from the article:

> Fifteen said that if they could avoid being detected they would cheat on income tax if the opportunity arose, keep any overchange a cashier or teller might give them, drink until they're potted if that's the mood of the party they are attending, keep an extra bag of groceries a supermarket clerk might hand them in mistake, seduce a lonesome girl and hold the boys spellbound by tales of such infidelities, hoodwink employers or customers by manipulations that amount to outright fraud and attempt to get ahead in their jobs at the expense of subordinates.
>
> The other five had only one reservation: they wouldn't cheat anyone who couldn't afford to be cheated.

All of the actions mentioned in this passage would be considered wrong when judged by the standards of morality that our society is alleged to subscribe to. Here then we have twenty people who either do not know that these actions are wrong, or do not know what it means to apply the term 'wrong' to a type of action, **or** who believe that the word 'wrong' means nothing more than 'disapproved by some or the majority of people in our society'. Here again we have evidence of what I mean by confusion and misunderstanding concerning the nature of morality.

The same article quotes an American writer, Robert E. Fitch, as saying that a number of modern intellectual movements "all converge in assisting a creeper crawler approach of relativism in ethics that soon becomes so absolute that after a while there are no longer any ethics on hand to be relativized". The context makes it clear that he was thinking of popular ideas derived from biology, sociology, psychology, and linguistic philosophy. I think it is true to say that much of the work done by various kinds of social scientists has been interpreted by the public at large as throwing serious doubt on the foundations of morality. The widespread diffusion of anthropological literature, now easily available in cheap paperback editions, has strengthened what is in fact a very old idea, namely: that all morals are relative and there are no absolute moral standards. This idea, which is hoary with antiquity, was familiar to Socrates in the fifth century B.C., but it has undoubtedly gained wider currency in the twentieth century now that it seems to have the blessing of modern science.

Some curious inferences about morality and moral education have also been drawn by amateurs from the work of professional psycho-analysts. An eminent psychologist, Dr J. C. Flugel, described the situation in the twenties and thirties of this century. He said:

> Were not some psycho-analysts hinting that the conventional inhibitions imposed by our moral standards were more than human nature could comfortably bear, and were not enthusiastic laymen on the strength of all this advocating the wholesale overthrow of restraint and discipline — in education, in the relations between the sexes, and in other spheres, so much so that parents were beginning to be afraid of exercising even the most elementary forms of control over their children lest in so doing they become guilty of producing repressions or neurotic symptoms.

Dr Flugel goes on to claim that psycho-analysts were not responsible for this misinterpretation of their work, but such misconceptions have deeply affected the methods of moral education adopted in this century. Many traditional moral beliefs have been undermined by hasty and ill-thought-out popularizations of the important work done by social scientists. Nothing systematic has been done to put sounder beliefs in their place. The result is general moral confusion. I don't intend here to discuss the bearing of the findings of the social scientists upon moral philosophy, which is clearly a matter of great importance. Moral progress does largely depend upon the growth of our factual knowledge both of human nature and of the world in which we live. However, my present concern is to describe the type and source of the confusion that centres on the idea of morality.

A further source of difficulty is the way in which people so often confuse morality with religion. In a society like our own, in which the dominant religion is an ethical one deeply concerned with both the spiritual and moral well-being of its adherents, this confusion is perhaps natural, but none the less misleading. Religion and morality may be related, but they are not identical. After all, even a thoroughly irreligious society — if such exists anywhere — would still have to have a morality if it were a society at all. And there are types of religion with almost no ethical content, where the emphasis falls almost exclusively upon ritual practice. The nature of the relation between morality and religion is an extremely difficult and highly controversial matter that raises complex philosophical problems. I shall touch on these at the end of this series of talks.

Yet another difficulty faced by the moral philosopher arises from the fact that the whole subject of morality tends to arouse fairly violent emotional reactions. On the one hand, the older generation — and this has been a kind of occupational disease among older people for centuries — the older generation claim to be shocked at what they call the lowering of moral standards among the young, and this state of shock makes it difficult for them to make the effort necessary to understand how morality strikes the young. Then there are those sensitive souls who find it quite shocking that anyone should engage in public discussion of anything so private and personal as they claim morality to be, and again their psychological state does not make for ease of discussion. Finally, there are those who profess to be surprised that anyone should take morality at all seriously in the twentieth century. Presumably the twenty persons polled by the

4   MORAL PHILOSOPHY

newspaper reporter would be in this state. If a person thinks that there is really nothing to discuss, that morality is a thoroughly outmoded idea, then discussion dies before it has even got under way; since discussion of any kind is an activity of reason, it demands a certain measure of emotional detachment at least during the period of discussion. When any subject by its very nature generates emotional reactions and a tendency to wishful thinking—and this is certainly true of morality—then those who discuss it must be prepared to be more than usually on their guard against those subjective influences that so easily tempt reason from its proper path. I say 'more than usually on their guard' because all thinking is continually subject to forces that tend to distort it. There are the traps set by language, which have occupied the attention of philosophers so much during the past twenty years. Psychologists and psychoanalysts have also done a great deal to make us aware of all manner of unconscious feelings and wishes that can mislead us. If we were to believe that all thinking, without exception, is necessarily distorted by unconscious factors, then indeed there would be little point in attempting a rational discussion of morality—or of anything else. Since this is absurd, we must adopt the only practical alternative of thinking as carefully as we can, making constant checks to make sure that we have not fallen into error, and submitting our thoughts to the criticism of other people. This is, of course, the method used by scientists in general, including psychologists—none of whom, so far as I know, have abandoned the study of psychology on the ground that all thinking is doomed to inevitable distortion. My immediate point is that the highly emotional nature of our subject-matter makes it necessary to be extra careful.

The last set of difficulties I want to mention concern more directly the task of the moral philosopher. Not only does the philosopher in general have to explain the nature of his subject and its methods, but the moral philosopher in particular must make it clear that he is *not* doing a number of things that he is frequently alleged to be doing. The moral philosopher is sometimes mistaken for the moralist, he is often confused with the moral teacher, and on occasion he is accused of being a moral preacher. A moralist is someone who seeks to draw a moral lesson either from an edifying story, from some event that has taken place, or from his observations on human behaviour. It is quite possible that someone listening to a moral philosopher may draw for himself a moral lesson from something that the philosopher has said or from an example he has used. But when this happens — and there is no reason why it should not happen — it is entirely accidental and forms no part of the philosopher's primary intention. The works of the great moralists like Bacon, La Rochefoucauld, or La Bruyère, are among the finest in our Western literature, but they are not specimens of moral philosophy. A moral teacher is a person whose express function is to inculcate a proper set of moral beliefs in the young. These teachers have an important role to play in any society. Without persons who were prepared to assume this role there would be no continuity in the moral tradition of society, indeed there would be no continuity in social life at all. However, the work of the moral philosopher, which consists largely in critical reflection on the grounds of moral beliefs, cannot even begin until long after the work of the moral teacher has been completed. In recent years philosophers appear to have been particularly afraid of being mistaken for preachers (i.e. people who exhort us to follow a way of life or live up to certain standards). This fear has its roots in the mistaken belief that philosophy should imitate the example of science and adopt a position of strict moral neutrality. If a philosopher decides for one solution to a problem rather than another, then he has abandoned the position of moral neutrality. However, if his position is supported by solid arguments, I see no reason why he should not do so. To present an argument is neither to exhort nor is it to give advice. It is to make an appeal to common human reason, the only authority recognized by a philosopher.

In this connection there is a possible source of misunderstanding that I would like to remove at once. Although the moral philosopher is engaged in discussing various moral rules and principles, he is most emphatically not concerned to lay down or establish a set of moral principles that must be recognized by everyone, nor does he attempt to formulate policy about the ends to be pursued by mankind at large. The moral philosopher is in no sense a moral legislator or a moral policy maker. Moral philosophers have indeed talked about establishing some principle of morality. Kant in the eighteenth century and John Stuart Mill in the nineteenth century were both concerned to establish moral principles. This is true, but we must be careful to understand the sense in which they were using the word 'establish'. Neither Kant nor Mill thought of themselves as establishing a new principle of morality in the way in which a body of legislators might enact or establish new laws, which the citizens would then have to obey. In arguing for the principle of the greatest happiness for the greatest number, Mill claimed that he was simply clarifying something that was implicit in the ordinary moral consciousness, but which had not yet been accurately formulated. In so doing he was engaged in critical analysis and reasoned argument designed to establish a conclusion. Kant not only stated that this was what he was doing, but he also poured scorn on a critic who had complained that his book contained no new principle of morality. "Who would think" Kant wrote "of introducing a new principle of all morality, and making himself as it were the first discoverer of it, just as if all the world before him were ignorant of what duty was or had been in thoroughgoing error." Both Kant and Mill — and to them we can add the names of their great Greek predecessors Plato and Aristotle — interpreted their task as moral philosophers to be that of careful analytic reflection on the morality of ordinary men and women, including themselves, with a view to separating the wheat from the chaff among moral beliefs by means of rational criticism. They did not legislate, they presented arguments for our consideration.

Before I can give you a positive description of the moral philosopher, I have still to distinguish him from yet another figure. The moral philosopher does not set himself up to be a moral expert. This is perhaps the most surprising among my denials and we must look at it more closely. Let us see what the expression 'a moral expert' means. Since morality is a practical business, a matter of doing what is right and avoiding what is wrong, we might say that the moral expert is someone who is unusually skilful both at knowing what ought to be done and at carrying it out even in the face of difficulties. There are such people, perhaps not very many of them, and they compel our admiration. We do not usually call them experts, but rather saints. If we called these people 'experts', we should be using the word as it is used in such phrases as 'an expert skier' or 'an expert rifle-shot', someone well trained and skilful in some practical activity. Although a philosopher might *wish t*o become a moral saint, he will not do so through his philosophy. Philosophy is largely a matter of argument, and Aristotle rightly observed a long time ago that "it is hard, if not impossible, to remove by argument the traits that have long since been incorporated in the character". This is why he also pointed out that no-one becomes a good man by attending lectures on moral philosophy. The way to goodness is both longer and harder.

According to the dictionary there is yet another sense of the word 'expert': "one whose special knowledge or skill causes him to be an authority". This is the sense in which we talk of an expert scientist or historian, one who has studied a subject long and thoroughly and who is therefore able to make authoritative pronouncements to the layman about problems lying within his special field. You might think that the moral philosopher, after a long period of training and experience in discussing moral problems, should be in a position to make authoritative pronouncements to the layman when moral problems arise. A brief glance at the major types of moral problems should dispel this illusion. In the first place, a man faces a moral problem when he knows perfectly well what he ought to do, but finds himself extremely disinclined to do it. Perhaps doing the right thing would involve him in personal sacrifice or will almost certainly hurt someone whom he has no desire to hurt. With one side of his nature he wants to do what is right, but with the other side he does not. This can be a very acute problem, but it is a very personal one requiring the man above all to come to grips with himself. If assistance can be given in such cases, it can only be through extending personal sympathy and encouragement. The philosopher may indeed do this, but in his capacity as fellow human being, not as professional philosopher.

Another common type of moral problem is that faced by the person who really does want to do what is right but finds him-

MORAL PHILOSOPHY

self in a highly complex situation where it is not at all obvious what the right thing really is. Or it may be that he finds himself in a situation where two of the moral principles that he has always regarded as binding have come into conflict, and he is uncertain which it is morally more important to follow. Faced with practical problems of this type, it is not unnatural for a man to seek assistance. If he admits his perplexity and asks to be told what to do, it is not necessary to find a philosopher to tell him that he cannot shift the responsibility of making up his own mind about what he ought to do onto the shoulders of someone else. If he describes his situation and asks for advice about what to do, then there are two points to be made. Firstly, to ask for advice about what to do is quite different from asking to be told what to do. Advice that is given need not be followed. If advice is accepted, then it is accepted because it is seen to be relevant to the situation. If it is rejected, it will be rejected because it does not fit the situation. Of course advice that is eventually rejected may none the less be of great assistance in the process of discovering what ought to be done. Secondly, when we seek advice about what to do in a difficult moral situation, the person to whom we turn is a man with considerable experience of life for whose personal moral integrity we have a high respect. It may be that a philosopher will answer this description, but, if he does, it will be because he has achieved the status of a morally upright person. And as Aristotle observed, he will have become that by practices other than philosophical argument. I am forced to conclude, therefore, that the moral philosopher cannot, in his capacity as a moral philosopher, be considered to be a moral expert in either of the two possible senses of that term.

If the moral philosopher neither moralizes nor preaches nor legislates nor functions as an adviser on practical moral problems, you may well begin to wonder just what he does do. Perhaps the simplest and the least misleading positive description I can give is to say that the moral philosopher seeks to understand and to interpret moral experience. In so far as understanding and interpreting are theoretical activities, his task is theoretical—like that of the physicist seeking to understand the behaviour of matter. But what distinguishes the moral philosopher from any kind of scientist, including the social scientist, is that he has to try to understand moral experience from the inside. He cannot make moral experience an object to which he can adopt a wholly detached attitude in the manner regarded as appropriate to a scientist. While examining moral experience, the philosopher remains a moral being, subject to all the usual duties and obligations characteristic of moral living and experience. Indeed it is only because this is so that he is in a position to try to understand moral experience. Moral experience itself is not something that can be caught and put under a microscope. It is something dynamic and constantly changing, something found only in the lives of actual persons. There is an important sense in which the practice of moral philosophy is a means to self-knowledge, and indeed the founder of the subject, Socrates, explicitly did regard it in that way.

An important consequence of this conception of the philosopher's task — and this is true for all branches of philosophy — is that every man must do his own philosophizing for himself. In this respect philosophy differs from either science or history. In order to read or learn about physics or history, I don't need to become a physicist or a historian. The results of the work of physicists and historians are to be found, partly at least, in the books they write. Those of us who are not professional physicists or historians more or less have to accept what they say on authority. But you may say "Isn't this true of philosophers who also have been known to write books?". The answer to that is quite emphatically "No". And the reason is that the philosopher is not concerned to state a number of facts about anything, facts that could be learnt or accepted on authority. He is concerned to understand, and understanding is an intensely personal activity. When a philosopher writes a book or makes any type of public utterance, what he is doing is inviting his readers or hearers to join him in the task of thinking about some aspect of human experience in the hope that through that activity of thinking some measure of understanding can be achieved. To join in that type of thinking *is* to philosophize. The professional philosopher is simply someone who has undergone specialized training in that kind of thinking. This joint activity of thinking is what is meant by philosophical discussion, which is why the method of philosophy is often known as the dialectical method, from the Greek verb *dialegesthai*, which means 'to discuss a problem'.

If this is what philosophy is, then the truth, accuracy, or acceptability, of what a philosopher says has to be tested and checked by the reader or hearer for himself by the reflective examination of his own experience. There is, I think, only one rule that must be observed by anyone who wishes to take part in this joint philosophical enterprise. What a philosopher says must never be accepted as obviously true or rejected as obviously false, without critical reflection. Uncritical agreement or disagreement are both equally worthless in the philosophical enterprise because to agree or disagree without first critically examining what has been said is simply not to think, and thinking is of the very essence of philosophizing.

Until quite recent times, the moral philosopher tried to state, expound, and defend, one of the recognized ethical theories. There are five general types of theory that are worth mention. Firstly, there is the oldest theory of all, *hedonism*, which seeks to account for all human moral effort in terms of the simple principle that pleasure is the sole good for man. Secondly, there are *utilitarian* theories, whose distinguishing mark is the belief that the rightness and wrongness of human actions is to be explained by reference to their results or consequences, which are judged as good or bad. Thirdly, there are theories that maintain that the ideas of rightness and obligation are fundamental and indeed the only ideas that can strictly be called moral. Theories of this kind are known as *deontological*, a word derived from the Greek word *deon* meaning 'that which is right'. Fourthly, there are *idealist* theories, which seek for the grounds of both the rightness of actions and the goodness of ends in their joint relation to whole patterns or ways of life. Fifthly, there are various kinds of *subjectivist* theories, which try to explain moral judgements as essentially subjective expressions of feeling or emotion.

During the twentieth century, philosophers in the English-speaking world have become more and more interested in the ways in which language affects our thinking. This has led to a new method in moral philosophy: the study of the language of morals. This method has undoubtedly clarified a number of problems, and it has set very high standards of linguistic accuracy in moral discussion. However, it is doubtful if by itself this method is wholly adequate. The language in which we express our moral ideas is certainly worthy of the most careful study; but to reach anything like a satisfactory understanding of moral experience we must penetrate beyond mere words and sentences to the experience itself. Language is indeed the glass through which we human beings view the world in which we live; but, as one philosopher has observed, "if we wish to see the landscape through the window, it is fatal to focus our eyes upon the window pane".

In the talks that follow I shall be concerned mainly to clarify what is meant by morality, moral experience, and moral judgement. It is hardly necessary to say that in the space at my disposal I have to be highly selective among the many problems that lie open to discussion and that even those that I do raise can only be briefly glanced at. The object of these talks, however, is not to close but to open discussion of some of the topics that belong to moral philosophy.

THE NATURE OF MORALITY

2

Since moral philosophy is an attempt to understand and interpret moral experience, our first step must be to identify just what it is that we are seeking to understand. What is referred to by such words as 'morality' or 'ethics' or such expressions as 'the moral consciousness' or 'moral experience'? The dictionary is of little help because what we want to find out is not how these words are used (by those who know how to speak English) but rather something about the nature of what these words and phrases refer to when they are being used. If I don't happen to know what an armadillo is, I shall find a phrase describing it in the dictionary. My understanding of what an armadillo is would be much increased by detailed accounts of its various habits, and very greatly increased if I were to have the experience of seeing and watching an armadillo for some time, that is: if I could penetrate beyond mere words to the world in which armadillos exist. Similarly, a verbal definition of morality will take us only a very short distance towards our goal. What we must do is identify that element in our experience to which the word 'morality' refers. Only then do we really know what we are talking about. There is a difficulty here, which we should note before we start. It is comparatively simple to get to know about things like armadillos, which can in fact be observed, which are objects that we can experience by means of our senses. The word 'morality', however, does not refer to any object that could be seen, touched, or smelt, or to anything that can be put under a microscope or on a dissecting table. It refers rather to a mode of experience, which is something considerably more complex than an object.

We can at least point to the general area where we might expect to find morality. Morality has something to do with human actions or human conduct, and more specifically it has to do with the fact that human beings have come to think of actions as being either right or wrong. This will do to begin with. Human beings not only act, they also have ideas about their actions, moral ideas, or moral beliefs, which they express from time to time in the form of moral sentences or judgements. It has been said — and correctly, I think — that human conduct is distinguished from mere animal behaviour by the presence of moral ideas. This distinction between behaviour and conduct is fundamental in moral philosophy. By 'behaviour' we mean any observable activity of a living creature. Conduct, on the other hand, while it is expressed in behaviour and is therefore to that extent observable — we certainly can observe what people do — conduct implies some attempt to regulate or control what is done in terms of either rules or standards. Conduct has been defined as the deliberately purposed actions of beings who possess moral ideas, who are aware, that is, of a distinction between right and wrong. At this point we must be very careful. When I say that human beings are aware of this distinction, I do not mean that they never have any difficulty in deciding which actions are to be called right and which wrong, and I do not mean that their ideas are necessarily correct. By awareness of the distinction I mean that they know the meaning of right and wrong and have some criteria for the application of these words. They know that a right action is one that ought to be done and that a wrong action is one that ought not to be done. They also have some concrete beliefs about the general kinds of actions that are right and wrong, and these will vary according to the type of moral education they have been given. Among widely accepted moral beliefs in our society today would be the belief that cruel actions and deceitful actions are wrong and that paying debts and keeping promises are right.

Anthropologists have studied different human societies with a view to discovering the nature of their moral customs and beliefs, a task that demands very careful methods of observation and interpretation. Their work leaves no doubt about two outstanding facts: human beings everywhere do have moral beliefs, and different societies have different moral beliefs. For example, in our society deliberate, indiscriminate lying is thought to be wrong, but in some Bantu tribes there is no moral stigma attached to lying except in special circumstances. Among the Chuckchee Indians a son has a moral duty to kill his father before he loses all vigour and vitality, an action we should regard as unthinkably wrong. Among the inhabitants of the island of Wogeo, off New Guinea, adultery with the wife of a man from another village is regarded as something to be proud of, while adultery with the wife of a fellow villager is morally condemned; we make no such fine distinctions in this area of conduct. The actual moral beliefs held by any society depend to some extent on the physical and economic conditions under which they live and also on their factual beliefs about the nature of the world. In this sense morality may be said to be relative. Whether it is relative in any other sense we cannot say until we have gone further in our analysis of all that is meant by the word 'morality'.

Since moral beliefs are beliefs about what ought to be done, we can expect them to be expressed in two ways: either in conduct itself or in the form of a linguistic utterance. People do quite frequently state their moral beliefs in the form of particular judgements such as "It was absolutely and utterly wrong of Hitler to order the extermination of the Jews" or "It was quite right of Sir Walter Scott to work hard in order to pay off his debts" or "I don't really want to go out tonight, but since I agreed to do that job at the canteen, I really ought to go there". Or moral beliefs can be expressed in the form of general statements such as "It is right to keep one's promises" or "One ought to pay one's debts" or "Cruelty is wrong" or "Bribery is wrong". However, it is not possible simply to assume that when a person *says* that certain types of action are wrong, he necessarily believes that they are wrong. A person may utter an insincere moral statement or he may simply repeat a moral statement that he has heard or been taught without really understanding it. The sincerity of a man's moral professions may be tested by observing how he acts. If a person sanctimoniously says that of course he thinks that to make a false statement is wrong and yet persistently falsifies his personal Income Tax return, we should have to conclude either that his statement was insincere or that he did not understand what it means to call a type of action wrong. There is also a third possibility here. He may really believe that making false statements is wrong but he may be too weak in the face of temptation to bring his own conduct into line with his beliefs. Precisely because they are modest about their own ability to live up to public utterances, many people are very reluctant to state their beliefs in actual moral sentences. However, it would be a serious mistake to infer that therefore they had no moral ideas. Their beliefs find expression in actual conduct.

Now, conduct may be judged morally from at least three different angles. An action may conform or fail to conform to some moral rule or principle. Rules of conduct of some kind are an essential feature of any organized society; for only if human beings are prepared to submit their conduct to regulation by rules is it possible to achieve that minimum degree of stability and order without which social co-operation would not exist. Moral rules have been described as the very stuff of the moral life, and I shall have more to say about them later. They are usually expressed in some such general form as "Never accept bribes" or "Always keep your promises"; and it is chiefly in connection with the way in which they conform or fail to conform to rules that actions are judged to be right or wrong. Then again, an action can also be looked at as a means of achieving some end or purpose. In this case its moral quality may be largely determined by the nature of the end, and ends are usually judged to be good or bad. I say *may* be determined by the nature of the end. There are occasions when the goodness of the end justifies the claim that an action is right, there are also many occasions when an action that would in fact realize a good end would none the less be judged to be wrong. The dictum that the end justifies the means is not a principle that can be universally accepted. An act of killing may eliminate a dangerous criminal, but if it is done by a private person, like Jack Ruby, the act is not likely to be regarded as morally right. In addition to the action and the end realized through the action, there is also the *way* in which the action is done, its inner aspect, its motive. It is extremely difficult to determine a motive—indeed Kant used to maintain that we can *never* be certain about this point. It is none the less true that in estimating a person's moral merit we try to take into account both the motive and the circumstances in which the action is done. When actions are judged from the point of view of the motive it is customary to refer to them as morally good or morally bad. Sometimes the moral merit of an action is estimated in terms of the effort of will demanded of the agent in doing it. There is a moral difference between the man who does what he ought to do because he happens to want to and the man who does what he ought to even when he would much prefer to be doing something else.

Since the eighteenth century another term has been prominent in moral discussion, the idea of duty. It is not uncommon for a person to express a particular moral belief by saying that he has a moral duty to do something, and moralists have attempted to draw up lists of different kinds of duties. Like other moral terms, the word 'duty' appears also in non-moral contexts. We speak about legal, military, or social duties. A duty is esssentially something that is expected of a man by virtue of some office he holds, position he occupies, or function he has to perform. We say that a parent has duties towards his children in the way of looking after them, seeing that they are fed, housed, and educated; or that a teacher has certain duties of teaching and administration. A duty is an action that we ought to perform, and in so far as it is a duty we ought to perform it whether we feel inclined to do so or not. A teacher ought to meet his classes at the appointed times even if he would rather be doing something else that morning. The duty arises from the fact that he is a teacher. A hostess must make herself pleasant to her guests even if she happens to dislike them personally. The fact that duty ought to be done irrespective of personal inclination has caused many moral philosophers to make it the central term in all discussions of morality. This is partly due to the influence of Kant, who did have a great deal to say about the motive of duty when he was analysing the concept of moral obligation. However, this practice leads to unnecessary difficulties; for the word 'duty' cannot properly be used to express everything that we morally ought or ought not to do. I can say that I ought not to steal, but it is stretching the meaning of the word to say that I have a duty not to steal. The central idea in morality, as we shall see, is not duty but what is expressed in the verb 'ought'.

So far, I have used the expression 'moral sentences' to refer to our overt utterances about moral affairs, but there is a long tradition in which the expression 'moral judgement' is used for the same purpose. This tradition is a little out of favour at the moment, largely because many contemporary philosophers have been more interested in discussing the purpose for which we make verbal utterances than in analysing their significance. However, the term 'judgement' seems peculiarly appropriate for expressing moral ideas. Let us look at some of the different types of moral judgement that people make. There are moral judgements made by a person who is in a situation where he has to *do* something, and these are known as agent judgements. In straightforward situations, the agent may not actually say anything but he will act in a manner that expresses his judgement. On other occasions he may have to do quite a lot of hard thinking before he can reach the point of saying "This is what I ought to do". In the light of all he knows about the situation he judges that one action rather than another is the right one for him. This is not unlike what we do when we have to judge some distance that we do not know and for some reason cannot actually measure. And when we judge, and don't merely guess, we can, if necessary, give the grounds for our judgement. This may be called the logical sense of the term. But there is more to it than that. When we judge that we ought to do something, we are not merely describing some proposed action, we are applying certain standards, norms, or criteria. And this bears some resemblance to what a judge does in a court of law. He pronounces his judgement in the light of what the law requires. Moral judgements about conduct are made in the light of standards or rules to which we subscribe. If I believe that promises ought to be kept, then I may judge that I ought to do some particular action because it would be a means of fulfilling a promise that I had made.

In addition to agent judgements, we also make several different kinds of spectator judgements, judgements about actions that have been done either by ourselves or by other people. We may come to recognize that something we have done in the past is wrong and we may admit it saying "Yes, I see now that it was wrong of me to do that". Or we may be called on to justify some action we have done; in which case we may say "I was quite right to do that because . . ." and then give our reasons. In these cases we are in the position of peculiarly privileged spectators since it is our own actions we are talking about. We also make spectator judgements about the conduct of other people. We may say about someone else that he ought not to have done something. We may judge that Hitler ought not to have sanctioned the use of torture against his political opponents. Sometimes people say that they don't want to sit in judgement upon what other people do. Since passing a moral judgement on the conduct of other persons is indeed a serious business, this is an understandable attitude. At the same time I think we must recognize that people do constantly make moral judgements about other people even if they do not always state them in very formal terms. A character in a recent novel is made to say "I don't want to make moral judgements, but that man's an absolute swine" — a quite devastating moral judgement expressed in highly colloquial terms. Then lastly, we are often asked to give moral advice by someone who finds himself in difficulty, and on some occasions we give it without being asked. Our judgement then takes the form "I think you ought to do so and so". There has been a great deal of controversy about the function of these advisory judgements, as we may call them, when they are uttered aloud. Philosophers who belong to the linguistic school, which I mentioned in my last talk, claim that such judgements are primarily intended to influence the other person to act in a certain way. While this may be true in some cases, it is certainly not true in all. It is quite possible that I may watch you doing something and at the same time think that what you are doing is wrong. Even though I remain silent, I am none the less making a moral judgement on your conduct. We do not always feel that it is appropriate to give utterance to all that we are thinking. When I do utter a judgement of the type "You ought to do so and so", I may indeed wish to influence you to do it, but I may also merely wish to draw your attention to factors in the situation that you may have missed. In that case I express my judgement in the hope that it will help you to see for yourself what it is that you ought to do.

We are now in a position to say with some confidence what the word 'morality' refers to. By the morality of any person or social group we mean primarily all the beliefs they hold about what actions are right or wrong and about what ends are worth pursuing. Since in journalistic usage the word 'morality' has come to be connected almost exclusively with what is right and wrong in sexual conduct, I want to emphasize as strongly as I can that morality covers all beliefs about what is right and wrong conduct in all human relationships. Moral philosophers sometimes use the term 'moral consciousness' as a synonym for morality in this sense. The word 'morality' is also used in a second sense to refer to the extent to which people live up to the moral beliefs that they profess to hold. A recent article in a popular weekly magazine bears the title 'What is happening to Canadian morality?'. The writer is not concerned about changes in moral beliefs about right and wrong but about a general failure to live up to recognized standards.

Our next task must be to see what we mean by the expression 'moral experience'. The word 'experience' itself has many meanings but let us consider the sense in which we talk about gaining experience as we go through life. The expression 'moral experience' will then include all that a man has been taught about morality, all the moral beliefs in terms of which he interprets moral situations; it will also include the ways in which his moral perception has been sharpened by accounts of moral situations in imaginative literature or in history, and finally all the accumulated recollection of moral situations in which he has had to make moral decisions, both his successes and his failures. This complex of beliefs and memories combine to produce a moral outlook upon life—this is what moral philosophy is concerned to examine, interpret, and criticize. The central feature in moral experience is the awareness of moral obligation. When a man faces the kind of situation that leads him to say "This is what I ought to do" then we say that he is aware of or is directly experiencing moral obligation. So far I have not raised any questions about what sort of actions we ought to do. I have mentioned as examples a number of types of action that people think they ought to do, such as paying their debts or keeping their promises, but I pointed out that the actual actions thought to be right or wrong will vary according to the type of society a man has been brought up in. *What* we ought to do is relative to the time and place in which we find ourselves. *That* there are certain actions that we ought unconditionally to do is what we might call the absolute element in morality.

The important word in that last sentence is the word 'unconditionally'. There are many occasions when the words "I ought to do such and such" do not express a moral judgement at all, but a prudential judgement. By a prudential judgement I mean a judgement concerning what will be in the agent's own interest. This may be his short-term interest or his long-term happiness. If I am a martyr to indigestion every time I eat lobster salad, then when it is offered to me I may judge that I ought not to eat it. The suffering that I anticipate on the basis of past experience does not appear to be worth the mild, present enjoyment of eating it. If we are asked to advise a young man on the choice of a career we might say to him that with his potentialities and special aptitudes he ought to choose law. Only through giving his capacities full rein in that direction do we judge that he is likely to be happy. In prudential judgements the 'ought' is grounded in what is thought to be in the agent's interest. Another way of putting this is to say that a prudential judgement has always got an *if*-clause attached to it—implicitly or explicitly—which expresses the agent's interest: "I ought not to eat lobster salad if I want to avoid indigestion"; "You ought to go in for law if, being the kind of person you are, you want to be happy". Prudential judgements are therefore conditional. On the other hand, when a man judges that some action is one that he ought morally to do, then part of his meaning is that the situation demands of him an action that takes precedence over his personal desires and inclinations. The moral 'ought' is unconditional or categorical. If a young man's father falls seriously ill, he may judge that it is his moral duty to carry on the family business. In claiming that it is his moral duty to do so, he indicates that there are elements in the situation that lead him to think that he must put to one side his personal inclinations, whatever they may be. The unconditional nature of the moral judgement means that it is an ultimate judgement from which there is no appeal to any higher authority.

Now, there is an ancient source of misunderstanding here, which we must clear out of the way. When I say that the moral judgement is ultimate and unconditional, that it takes precedence over personal inclinations, I do not mean that every time we make a moral judgement about what we ought to do we must be doing something that is opposed to our inclinations. For some curious reason many people have thought that this is what moral philosophers have meant. In consequence a great deal of nonsense has been written about the grim austerity of the moral life. In actual fact what we morally ought to do is very often what we want to do in any case. The young man who judges it his moral duty to carry on the family business may be quite glad to have the opportunity to do so. It is a parent's duty to look after his children, but the average parent wants to do that anyway. Of course, it is important that we should not allow the influence of a strong desire to distort our judgement about what we ought to do. This certainly can happen; for practical judgements are more open to distorting pressure from desires and inclinations than are theoretical judgements. This illustrates what I said in my first talk about the need for extra care in thinking about morality. The danger of rationalization is real, but provided we are aware of it we need not succumb to it. However, duty does sometimes run counter to inclination. It is when it does that we become most acutely aware of the reality of moral obligation.

Some philosophers have argued that when we say a man is under a moral obligation to do something we mean that he is bound under penalties to do it, that if he fails to fulfil his moral obligations he will suffer for it. Now, *legal* obligations are created by the law, and no law could be regarded as valid if it were habitually disregarded by the community at large. To give the law teeth, as it were, legislators generally add to the law threats of penalties for violation. The ultimate reason why we obey the law is not of course fear of punishment, but it is surely a fact that a strong motive towards obeying the law may very often be our knowledge that violation carries penalties. Many people obey the law about speeding on the highway only when they know there is a police cruiser in the vicinity. It is also quite true that if a man does something that runs counter to the accepted moral standards of the community, other people may cause him to feel their disapproval in all sorts of unpleasant ways. There certainly are moral and social sanctions as well as legal ones. The point at issue is this. When we say "I ought morally to do such and such" or "I am under a moral obligation to do such and such" do we mean simply that if we fail to do the action in question we shall meet with the moral disapproval of the other members of our society? Is the statement "I ought to do such and such" merely a disguised prediction about the behaviour of other people towards us? Many people have argued this view at great length, but I want to make only two points. Firstly, it is possible to say "I (or you) ought to do such and such" when we know perfectly well that no unpleasant consequences are at all likely to ensue. If I make a promise to a dying man when no one else is present, I can break it without any fear of meeting the disapproval of others, for no one will know I am breaking it. However many people, including myself, would hold that, in the absence of unexpected moral complications, the promise still ought to be kept. Secondly, it is possible for a man to judge that he ought to do something in the full knowledge his action will not meet with general approval. This is the kind of situation the moral reformer finds himself in. Unless we are going to hold that our moral standards simply could not be improved, we must recognize that this situation is possible. There have been moral reformers in the past who, by taking a moral stand against the accepted views of the community, have brought the rest of us to see moral aspects of certain situations to which we had been blind. At one time our own ancestors could see no serious moral objection to a situation in which one man literally owned another as his personal slave. Through the devoted efforts of a series of reformers we have come to hold strong views condemning slavery as immoral.

The experience of moral obligation is the central element in the concept of morality. Precisely because it does sometimes run counter to our inclinations, people have tried to explain it away, and such attempts will doubtless continue. Anyone who examines his moral beliefs in an unprejudiced manner is likely to discover that he does, even if only occasionally, find himself faced with an unconditional moral obligation. If he claims that he does not, then neither I nor anyone else can prove that there is such a thing. If moral obligation is real, then like anything else that is real, it cannot be proved. It can only be experienced. All that can be done is to remove possible sources of confusion in speaking about it. Every man must discover the fact of moral obligation for himself within his own experience. I would like to conclude this talk by saying that if moral obligation is some kind of illusion, then morality itself is an illusion, and we should have to regard human society as having no more solid basis than mutual fear between man and man. Without morality human life would indeed be as Hobbes observed, "poor, nasty, brutish, and short".

HOW MORAL JUDGEMENTS ARE MADE   3

In my last talk I was chiefly concerned to explain what morality is, how it makes demands on us. But I did not touch upon the question "How do we come to know *what* demands it makes?". This is the next subject for investigation. Our problem can be stated in various ways, all of which in the end amount to the same thing. Let us take it in this form. Admitting that we make a distinction between right and wrong actions, how do we come to know which are right and which are wrong?

There is one general and traditional answer to this question, which I will discuss first. It is often said that we can consult conscience. "Do what your conscience tells you and you can't go wrong." At one time this was popular advice; and the expression 'to have a bad conscience' is still a common way of referring to the uncomfortable feelings we experience when we recognize that we have done something wrong or are neglecting some duty. To act against conscience is regarded as a fairly certain way of going wrong. Conscientious objectors, for example, are people whose personal moral principles will not allow them to follow some line of action generally accepted by others.

How then shall we describe this thing to which we give the name 'conscience'? Conscience is a moral notion that did not exist at the time of the classical Greeks, but which first came into our Western vocabulary through the writings of the Roman Stoics. Later it was taken up and developed by the early Christian writers, who described it in a powerful metaphor as the voice of God planted within the human breast. The great eighteenth-century moralist Joseph Butler described it in these words:

> We have a capacity of reflecting upon actions and characters, and making them an object to our thought; and on doing this we naturally and unavoidably approve some actions, under the peculiar view of their being virtuous and of good desert; and disapprove others as vicious and of ill desert. That we have this moral approving and disapproving faculty is certain from our experiencing it in ourselves and recognizing it in each other.

These words suggest that conscience is no special faculty, but simply a word used to indicate that we do pass moral judgements on human conduct. However, there is more to it than that. In ordinary usage my conscience can pass judgement on my actions and can make me extremely uncomfortable if I violate its orders, but *my* conscience cannot pass judgement on *your* actions and happily my conscience does not keep *me* awake at night in a high state of discomfort because *you* have acted wrongly. A man's conscience is concerned only with his own conduct.

Philosophers and psychologists have advanced various theories about the nature of conscience. Firstly, it has been suggested that conscience is a sentiment or mode of feeling. This theory probably arises from the experiences described as a good or a bad conscience, which are certainly states of feeling of some kind; but this will not account for the way in which we talk about conscience as a source of moral knowledge. Secondly, it has been identified quite simply with reason, reason directed upon problems of conduct. According to this view conscience yields knowledge or beliefs about the rightness and wrongness of general types of actions. For example, a person may say that his conscience told him that lying is wrong. Thirdly, conscience has been likened to a kind of moral sense, in which case it is concerned with individual situations and will pronounce particular judgements such as "You ought to do this now" or "You ought not to have done that yesterday". It seems to me more correct not to identify conscience with any one of these views, but to recognize that what we mean by conscience is something complex within which we can distinguish three strands of meaning. To say that we have a conscience means that we do in fact make moral judgements on our own behaviour, that we have a disposition to feel certain emotions in connection with the performance of certain actions, and that we have an active tendency to do actions judged right and avoid actions judged wrong.

The question now inevitably arises, is conscience something innate or is it something that we acquire through education? If by innate we mean that we arrive on earth with our minds fully stocked with ready-made moral judgements, then there is no evidence at all for such a view. On the other hand, if we simply mean that we have a capacity for moral reflection, which can be developed by training and education, just as our power of speaking and our power of reasoning are trained and developed, then conscience may be regarded as innate. However, the content and mode of action of this innate capacity has to be developed through education. Both moralists and psychologists have offered various descriptions of the way in which conscience is educated.

Although there is difference of opinion about details, there is fairly general agreement today that conscience must be educated. But if conscience has to be educated, it follows that what a man's conscience bids him do will vary according to the type of education he has received. Conscience may indeed represent within us the voice of the community but only in so far as those responsible for our education interpreted correctly the moral views of the community. This means that there is no ground for maintaining that conscience is an infallible guide to right conduct. The phrase 'my conscience' is simply a compendious way of referring to my moral beliefs about right and wrong so far as they apply to my own conduct. And these beliefs are as liable to error as any other human beliefs.

In this connection there is one much-debated question that we must consider. Is it ever right to go against conscience? Can conscientious action ever be wrong? If conscience is not infallible, then even when I follow the bidding of conscience it is possible that I may be doing wrong. This thought frightens many people who have always relied implicitly on the guidance of conscience. However, there are situations where conscience simply refuses to give any clear guidance at all, and there is also the problem posed by the fact that your conscience may not agree with mine. During the last war, I knew a number of young men whose consciences forbade them to take any part in warfare. They were people for whose moral integrity I had the utmost respect, and they followed the bidding of conscience at considerable cost to themselves. My own conscience did not forbid me, but on the contrary urged me in precisely the opposite direction. Were they right to do what they did? Or was I right? Or can the problem be formulated in such simple, black-and-white terms?

Let us look at an example of contemporary conscientious action. A young man, convinced that the use of nuclear weapons is radically evil, may believe quite sincerely that the only right thing for him to do is to become an active member of some 'Ban the Bomb' group. Many young people today are in precisely that situation and they defend their stand with zeal and sincerity. They are doing what they honestly believe to be right. Now, since they are ordinary, fallible human beings, it is possible that their moral interpretation of the situation is mistaken. Many people do think that they are misguided. The question I am asking is whether in that case we should say that what they are doing is morally wrong. I am not concerned just now with the rights and wrongs of 'Ban the Bomb' movements. I am using this example merely to give point to the general question, is it ever wrong to do what, following conscience, you sincerely believe to be right?

This kind of situation is common enough, and it forces us to recognize a new dimension of complexity in moral judgement. In some simple situations we may face a straightforward choice between right and wrong when there is no element of serious doubt. But in many situations there can be genuine doubt and sincere disagreement about what is right and wrong. We may say in such cases "I think that what you're doing is wrong, but I appreciate that you really believe that it's right, so I can't entirely blame you". We don't regard the situation as a total moral loss: there is something on the credit side. Even if the man is mistaken in his views, he is still acting from a morally impeccable motive, indeed one of the highest possible motives: the desire to do what is right. Some philosophers have suggested that we distinguish between the rightness and the moral goodness of an action. This means analysing the action into the public, observable act and the inner motive. Even when an act is wrong we may still judge that the whole action is morally good if the motive is the desire to do what is right. But there is a difficulty to bear in mind. It is very hard to be sure what motive does lie behind an action. We cannot even be sure what our own motives are in some cases. This means that judging the moral goodness of an action will be a much riskier business than judging whether an act is right. But unless we are prepared to take this distinction into account, we cannot hope to do justice to the real complexity of this type of situation.

Since it is plain fact that we do make moral judgements about the past and present conduct of other people as well as our own, we must broaden the limits of our discussion to include all kinds of moral judgement. Let us now divide moral judgements into two main types, general and particular. The general will include all judgements about types of actions such as "Breaking a promise is wrong" or "Paying one's debts is right". Particular moral judgements will refer to what is done in some quite particular situation, judgements such as "John did wrong in breaking that promise to Mary" or "Tom ought not to have taken that money. It didn't belong to him".

There does not seem to be any doubt that, for the most part, general moral judgements about the rightness and wrongness of types of actions are derived directly from moral teaching inculcated in our early years by parents and elementary-school teachers, and, in a society that adheres to an ethical religion, by religious authorities. These general moral beliefs are acquired not only through overt instruction in moral rules and principles but also through our natural human tendency to imitate and accept established modes of behaviour. Moral education, in short, proceeds through precept and example supplied by the authorities who surround us in our early years. There is nothing surprising in this; for it is how we acquire all our elementary knowledge about the world in which we live—our historical, geographical, and scientific knowledge. We accept on authority what is taught to us; and in our early days there is no reason why this should not be so. It is when people reach years of maturity without having begun to ask questions and to demand reasons for what they have been taught that we should lament the failure of our educational methods. At first, however, we accept moral teaching, like any other teaching, on authority. It provides us with the initial set of moral ideas with which we set out upon life. Moral maturity, like intellectual maturity, can be achieved only if at some time or another we seek to discover reasons for at least some of the moral beliefs that we have been taught. To investigate the foundations of moral belief is not to invite moral scepticism. On the contrary, it is only beliefs for which we have examined the reasons that we are likely to hold with any degree of conviction. This process of examining our moral beliefs may, and indeed generally will, result in some modification in the form of the beliefs with which we started. A person may set out on life believing firmly the universal rule that lying in any form is always wrong, but may come to hold the modified belief that lying is in general wrong but may in certain circumstances be morally justifiable.

Assuming then that it is through a more or less systematic form of instruction that we acquire our initial moral beliefs, we now have two very different questions to face. Firstly, what grounds can we have for believing that the moral beliefs we inherit are sound and reliable? Is there such a thing as moral knowledge or are all moral judgements in the end mere matters of opinion? This is a complex and very important problem, which I want to discuss in some detail in a later talk. Secondly, how, starting with an equipment of general moral beliefs, do we come to make particular moral judgements, and, more particularly, on those occasions when we are required to justify our judgement or when the right or obligatory action is not at all obvious? Let us look now at this second question.

Although I shall now be chiefly concerned with moral judgements as they are articulated in language, I think we should be careful not to forget that in ordinary, day-to-day living the vast majority of our moral ideas receive immediate expression in what we do, without passing through the stage of linguistic expression — to such an extent that we easily forget how pervasive the moral element in life really is. People don't usually formally announce to themselves in bed in the morning that they *ought* to get up in time to be at their work at the appointed hour. They simply do it, and because it is so commonplace they are barely aware that they are complying with a moral demand. It is generally when we run counter to our accepted moral ideas that we become most aware of them.

Moral judgements on particular actions or situations appear to be fairly immediate in form and are generally expressed in vague but often colourful language. We say "I don't like the feel of that proposal of yours" or "I just couldn't do that, it's against my principles". In so far as we are engaged in the practical business of living, we don't usually have to enlarge upon these immediate judgements, which arise directly out of the set or direction given to our moral thinking by our early training. One of the more acute among nineteenth-century philosophers, F. H. Bradley, described very well what happens: "If a man is to know what is right," he said "he should have imbibed by precept, and still more by example, the spirit of his community, its general and special beliefs as to right and wrong, and, with this whole embodied in his mind, he should particularize it in any new case . . ." We particularize, as Bradley puts it, in new cases without necessarily being able to produce our stock of general moral beliefs for inspection. A character in a contemporary novel makes the point very clearly, speaking for the ordinary person:

> there's practically nothing that you could ask me that I could tell you was right or wrong just — just by itself. But if you put me where it was all happening, I'd tell you fast enough whether it was right or wrong from the feel of it.

Now, while this is, I think, a good description of the actual way in which we make our day-to-day moral judgements, there are occasions when our judgement is challenged. Someone has declared that if Jane does that, then she will be doing wrong. Jane, let us say, has found that the sales clerk has forgotten to put a $3.00 item on her bill, and Jane proposes simply to keep the article and do nothing about it. Why, we may be asked, do we think that Jane would be doing wrong? We might reply by pointing out that Jane's conduct would be a form of theft, and theft is wrong. The immediate judgement that Jane's conduct is wrong now appears as the conclusion in an argument: theft is wrong, Jane's action would be a form of theft, so Jane's action is wrong. We defend our judgement by appealing to a general rule or principle that is taken to be sound.

It is possible, however, that this answer may not satisfy our questioner; and there are two points that he can now proceed to make. He can say "I agree that theft is wrong, but what makes you think that what Jane is doing is any kind of theft?". That is, he can challenge our identification of Jane's actual, particular action with the general type of action known as theft. The argument may proceed by an attempt to define theft; and if Jane's action cannot be called theft once a definition has been agreed upon, then, if we still think she is doing wrong, we can follow a similar line of argument and say that if it is not theft, it is still a form of dishonesty, and dishonesty is wrong. Or, our questioner may take quite a different line and say "Oh yes, I can see that if theft is wrong, Jane's conduct is wrong, but, what makes you think that theft is wrong?". That is, he can ask us to justify our belief that there is a moral rule forbidding theft. In ordinary life, this second type of question is probably much less common than the first. Most everyday arguments are of the first type and turn on whether some particular action can be considered to be a case of some general type. Few people would disagree outright with the principle that theft is wrong, but many people do things that appear suspiciously like theft, justifying themselves by arguing that their action is not really theft.

If our questioner pushes us to defend our view that theft is wrong, that there is a valid moral rule against theft, how would we proceed? Obviously, no one makes or obeys rules simply for the love of doing so. We feel that behind any rule of action there must be a reason for it. There have been three main ways in which philosophers have attempted to deal with this problem. The deontologists, as they are called, maintain that statements of the form "Theft is wrong" or "Lying is wrong" are self-evidently true. Statements of that type do not, they claim, need either proof or justification. Anyone who understands what

MORAL PHILOSOPHY

theft is, or what lying is, can see that these actions are wrong. This answer has not been universally accepted, although, in all fairness, it must be admitted that the analyses and arguments produced in support of it have often been in themselves extremely illuminating. The Utilitarian philosophers look to consequences in order to establish the rightness or wrongness of conduct. They argue that moral rules are to be justified in terms of the consequences that may be anticipated if they are generally obeyed. One consequence of having a rule against lying is that we can trust the word of our fellow men and this is a better state of things than if lying were general and we could never safely believe what was said to us. Similarly, we can justify having a rule against theft by pointing out that only with such a rule in force can we hope to be left in the enjoyment of our own personal property, and again this is judged to be good. This is indeed a very plausible line of defence, and on the surface it does not look very different from the third line of argument advanced by the Idealist philosophers. According to the Idealists, any given rule is to be justified by showing that it is a necessary condition of a whole way or pattern of life. This pattern will include a series of more or less closely interrelated rules. It will also include a complex collection of various good ends, which are partly made possible by the observance of the rules. To develop either the Utilitarian or the Idealist method of justifying moral rules in anything like the detail necessary to do them justice would take us far beyond the limits of these talks. For our immediate purpose it will be sufficient to note that both the Utilitarian and the Idealist answers imply that moral rules or general moral judgements about types of right and wrong action can ultimately be justified only in terms of judgements about what is good or bad. While moral rules appear to be an essential feature of the moral life, the foundations of morality must be looked for, not in the rules themselves, but in the kind of life made possible by general observance of the rules. The rightness of actions must be justified by reference to the common good or the goodness of a whole way of life.

As long as we can show that some particular act that we have judged to be right comes under some rule that itself can be justified by reference either to its consequences or its place in a way of life, there is no great difficulty in answering the question, how do we know what is right. However, the picture changes radically when we examine a rather different situation. Sometimes, when we are not sure what the right thing is, we find that we are faced with a conflict between fundamental rules. I am inclined to doubt whether this happens quite as often as some moral philosophers seem to suggest, but I am quite certain both that it does occur and that when it occurs it may represent a major crisis in a person's moral life. The resulting uncertainty has been described as "the profoundest and most terrifying species of moral uncertainty". Like all crises, the outcome may take several different forms. When the conflict occurs in the life of someone who up to that point had accepted unquestioningly the validity of the rules that he had been taught in childhood, it can produce great bewilderment and a feeling of "Where do I turn now?". The conflict may start him on that process of general moral reflection that leads to moral maturity. On the other hand, the inner tension induced by this discovery may prove too great and a pathological state may result. Psycho-analysts report many cases of neurotic and psychotic breakdowns that have been caused by moral stress. The passage I quoted in my first talk by Dr. Flugel indicates that some people have drawn from this the curious inference that no one should be taught to observe any rules, that we should impose no restrictions on the conduct of children, lest later on they develop a neurotic or psychotic condition. This can hardly be treated as a very serious argument. Logically it is on a par with arguing that because some people get killed on the highways in motor accidents, no one should be allowed to drive motor vehicles. Children certainly should be educated, both morally and intellectually, with the greatest care, but to attempt to wrap them in moral cotton wool as a possible protection against later dangers is simply to deny them the right to develop into mature human beings. Of course there will be casualties by the way. There always have been—both physical, intellectual, and emotional. Life cannot be lived without risk, and this is as true of the moral life as of any other form.

What then is the answer to this kind of situation? Let me mention some of the solutions that have been proposed. Firstly, there is the most naïve of all, that of the nineteenth-century Utilitarians. They suggested that when rules conflict we should decide upon the rightness of particular actions by estimating their probable consequences. This would require us to perform an act of moral and factual calculation well beyond the power of any normal human being. Secondly, there is the somewhat complacent answer of those philosophers who have concentrated their whole attention on the validation of the general moral rules; these deontologists claim that when our fundamental principles come into conflict we must examine the whole situation as fully as we can, both the facts of the situation and also the various moral principles thought to be involved, until we find the conviction forming within us that to follow one rather than another of the rules is morally more important. I have no doubt that in fact a conviction of that type would form itself in our mind, given enough time, but the problem, to which these moralists offer no solution at all, is how we would justify that conviction. There can be no appeal to a higher principle because the principles that have come into conflict are ultimate principles. And since these thinkers also hold that ultimate moral principles are themselves self-evidently true, they are debarred from justifying the decision by reference to anything beyond the principles. Thirdly, there is the attitude of the existentialists who make much of these fundamental conflicts between ultimate principles. Faced with the conflict, they claim, we find ourselves on the edge of a veritable abyss, the contemplation of which fills us with a species of moral vertigo. We become oppressed by a sense of how completely arbitrary are all fundamental moral choices. We must choose, for we must act, but we appear to have no grounds for our choice. We have to make a leap in the dark based not on reason but on faith. The existentialists must be given credit for emphasizing the emotional significance of moral conflicts, but I don't think we need accept their claim that the choice we are forced to make is completely groundless or entirely arbitrary. It is true that we cannot achieve mathematical certainty in our processes of deliberation. In practical affairs mathematical certainty never is attainable and we have to be content with rational probability, which, as Joseph Butler observed, is the guide of life. Only if arguments have no bearing at all on the choice we make can we say that our choice has been reduced to a lottery. And this brings us to the fourth solution, that of the Idealists. They fully admit the difficulties inherent in this kind of ultimate choice, but maintain that what we must do — for it is all we can do — is try to consider what is achieved by each of the conflicting rules within the pattern and fabric of social life, and then follow the one that we judge to be most important.

A very large part of moral philosophy consists in examining the grounds on which these different theories are based. This tends to be a lengthy and slow process of analysis. But in the course of it we become familiar with various kinds of moral situations and with a great variety of moral reasons for action. In this way we come to understand the nature of moral experience, which, as I said in my first talk, is the object of moral philosophy.

SUBJECTIVIST THEORIES

4

In the talks so far we have been considering the nature of morality. To do this we have been examining moral judgements. We have treated moral judgements as if, like any other judgements, they could be true or false. According to some contemporary theories, however, moral judgements are not judgements at all, but either expressions of feeling or attempts to influence the feelings and conduct of other persons. These subjectivist theories, as they are called, have been put forward in all seriousness by philosophers who certainly could not be accused of intending to undermine the foundations of morality. They have been motivated by sheer intellectual desire to find a satisfactory explanation of what it is that happens when a person makes a moral judgement, or, as they prefer to say, utters a moral sentence. The Emotive theory in particular has aroused a great deal of controversy, both among professional philosophers and among laymen. Since it has been one of the most widely discussed among twentieth-century ethical theories, we should at least see what it is and what kind of arguments have been brought forward both for and against it.

To understand the origins of the Emotive theory we must go back in time to the early thirties of this century in Vienna when a group of scientists with an interest in philosophy developed a general philosophical theory that came to be known as Logical Positivism. The adherents of this movement devised a theory of meaning based on what they called the Verification Principle. In this theory, statements were divided into three classes: firstly, the special kind of statements found in mathematics and logic, known as tautologies as they are true by definition (to these we need pay no further attention, for they do not enter the argument); secondly, genuine empirical statements, which express observable facts; and thirdly, nonsensical statements, which do not express any facts and strictly have no literal meaning. Genuine statements expressing facts were to be distinguished from nonsensical or pseudo-statements by applying the Principle of Verification. A statement had genuine meaning if it was possible to verify it by some form of sensible observation. This meant that the statements of both theology and morality were all nonsensical, because it is not possible, in the strict sense of 'observe', to observe any of the things referred to by theological or moral terms. Although we can observe the redness of an object, we cannot observe by means of any of our senses the rightness of an action. When we use moral language, when we make moral judgements, according to this theory, we are not literally saying anything, we are merely evincing certain feelings or giving expression to certain emotions of approval or disapproval. I should like to quote the words of one of the more distinguished English exponents of the theory, Professor A. J. Ayer:

> Thus if I say to someone, "You acted wrongly in stealing that money" I am not saying anything more than if I had simply said "You stole that money". In adding that this action is wrong I am not making any further statement about it. I am merely evincing my moral disapproval of it. It is as if I had said, "You stole that money" in a peculiar tone of horror, or written it with the addition of some special exclamation marks. The tone, or the exclamation marks, add nothing to the literal meaning of the sentence. It merely serves to show that the expression of it is attended by certain feelings in the speaker.

Professor Ayer goes on to say that

> If now I generalize my previous statement and say "Stealing is wrong" I produce a sentence which has no factual meaning, that is, expresses no proposition which can be either true or false. It is as if I had written

"Stealing money!!!" — where the shape and thickness of the exclamation marks show, by a suitable convention, that a special sort of moral disapproval is the feeling that is being expressed.

He concludes that "It is clear that there is nothing here which can be true or false".

It follows from this theory that it is impossible for any two people to disagree about an ethical statement — because there are no ethical statements to disagree about. If I say that Hitler was wrong to destroy people by using gas chambers, or that cruelty to small children is wrong, and someone else asserts that Hitler was right or that cruelty is perfectly permissible, then we are not in disagreement about modes of conduct. It is just that he happens to have different feelings about the two actions from those that I have. Obviously there is some truth in the theory. We do have feelings, and sometimes very strong feelings indeed, about certain types of actions. Some people have strong feelings about deliberate cruelty to children. Many might say that this is at least partly because they think that cruelty is wrong. But if the Emotive theory were correct, it would not make sense to say that. On this theory "Cruelty is wrong" is a pseudo-statement and merely indicates that the speaker happens to have strong moral feelings, and nothing more. It is important here that we distinguish between the perfectly innocuous statement "I have strong moral feelings about cruelty to children", which is a statement of fact about me, and the pseudo-statement "Cruelty to children is wrong", which on this theory states no fact of any kind; it merely *expresses* feeling in much the same way that "Ouch" expresses my feelings if you happen inadvertently to stand hard on my toe.

In this early version of the Emotive theory, which emphasizes the way in which ethical terms express emotion, there appears to be no difficulty in explaining any form of 'ought' statement. If I say either "I ought to keep my promises" or "You ought to pay your debts" or "He ought not to be cruel to his children", in each case I am simply expressing my feelings of approval about promise-keeping, and debt-paying, and of disapproval about cruelty. It is rather as if when I thought of promise-keeping I shouted "Hurrah" and when I thought of cruelty to children I said "Boo". Indeed among its opponents the theory was irreverently known as "The Boo-Hurrah theory of ethics".

The positivist approach to language led many philosophers to talk about two functions of language: the descriptive function and the emotive function. Putting it very roughly, we may say that language is used descriptively when there is a nice hard fact out there in the real world, which can be described. If I say "The book is red" then both the word 'book' and the word 'red' have what might be called an objective reference. There is a book and it is red and I am describing that fact. When on the other hand, I say "The book is good" the situation is alleged to be very different. The word 'book' has an objective reference, but the term 'good' does not. According to Ogden and Richards, two influential exponents of this general view, "Good serves only as an emotive sign expressing our attitude to (the book) and perhaps evoking similar attitudes in other persons, or inciting them to actions of one kind or another". This means that the sentence "This book is good" has to be understood as meaning something of this nature: "I like this book, read it please, and like it too." It is no longer a statement about the book, but about me and my desire that you should like it as well.

In its very crude original form, however, the theory did not satisfy anyone for long and it was subjected to very skilful refinement. When Professor Ayer first stated the theory in his book *Language, Truth and Logic*, he also said that "It is worth mentioning that ethical terms do not serve only to express feeling. They are calculated also to arouse feeling, and so to stimulate action". In the second stage of the theory philosophers began to attend to this 'persuasive' or 'dynamic' aspect of moral terms. They claimed that a major function of moral sentences was to persuade other persons to share the moral attitudes that we find in ourselves. This function is partly made possible by the emotive power of ethical terms like 'right' and 'wrong', 'good' and 'bad', and 'ought'. A sentence such as "Promise-keeping is right" has to be analysed into the two parts, "I approve of promise-keeping, pray do so too". Professor Stevenson, the chief advocate of this version, explicitly maintained that ethical judgements look to the future, that is, they are intended to influence action. There are still no genuine moral statements that we could agree or disagree about. On the other hand, it is possible to have a difference of attitude; and this was interpreted as a form of disagreement. I shall come back to this point later.

Now, this Emotive theory certainly does seem to account for some features of moral judgement, but there are some difficulties about it that we should note. In both the forms that I have mentioned, when a man says "Cruelty is wrong" or "You ought not to act in a cruel manner" he is not saying anything that could be true or false. What looks grammatically like a statement is a pseudo-statement, and it is used in order to influence the feelings of others or to express one's own feelings. What gives the theory its initial aura of plausibility is that moral sentences do often express emotion and are often used in order to influence people to feel or act in certain ways. But even so, the theory is still a long way from being convincing. Sentences other than moral sentences express emotion and are used in order to influence people and yet they retain an element that could be true or false. The simple statement "I just love ice-cream" can express feeling and also be true. If you happen to be passing an ice-cream shop with a small boy who says "I like ice-cream", you would be thought unusually stupid even for a grown-up if you treated that statement as nothing more than a piece of gratuitous information. It is an utterance designed to influence your conduct: to persuade you to buy him some ice-cream. It is indeed an oblique way of making his point, but surely no more oblique than moral sentences would have to be. For according to the Emotive theory we indulge in the complicated process of constructing sentences that look like statements but are not statements, simply in order to express our feelings. The fact that a sentence *can* be used as a means both of expressing feeling and of influencing conduct does nothing at all to show that it does not also *say* something, that it does not also have a literal meaning.

At this point we may begin to wonder whether the general theory of meaning from which the Emotive theory was derived is itself sound. There are two difficulties in that theory that I would like to mention. In the first place, it looks as if there is a confusion between the meaning and the truth of a statement. If we take the statement "There are men on the moon", we are told that the meaning of this statement lies in the method by

which it is verified. Now, the method of verifying that statement would involve making a lengthy journey into space and
exploring the whole surface of the moon to make sure that men
were in fact inhabiting it. The obvious difficulty is that we could
not even begin this process of verification unless we first of all
knew what the statement meant. And yet the theory claimed that
we can distinguish genuine statements, which have meaning,
from nonsensical statements only by applying the Principle of
Verification. Furthermore, not only is the theory hazy about
the difference between meaning and truth, it also seems to be
built on a confusion between two different senses of the word
'meaning'. If my wife is arranging a dinner party and I happen
to say "You know, I don't like Mr. X" she may interpret my
remark to mean not only that in fact I do dislike Mr. X but also
that I do not want him invited to the party. If in reply she
actually says "You mean you don't want me to invite him", she
is using the word 'mean' in the perfectly idiomatic sense of 'is a
sign that'. This sense is found in a statement such as "There's
smoke coming out of the chimney. That means someone is at
home". In one sense of 'mean' the first sentence just means what
it says, that there is smoke coming out of the chimney; but in the
other sense, the smoke is taken to be a sign of someone's presence.
My statement "I don't like Mr. X" has meaning in *both* senses
as my wife very well knows. Now, when I say "Cruelty to
children is wrong" that utterance on my part may be taken as a
sign that I have strong feelings against cruelty to children; what
the Emotive theory fails to do is to show convincingly that it
does not also have meaning in the first or literal sense.

The Emotive theory appears to be successful in dealing with
statements of the type "Promise-keeping is right" or "Promises
ought to be kept", where both the words 'right' and 'ought' are
interpreted as having strong emotional associations. At first
sight particular moral sentences such as "You ought to keep that
promise you made to your mother" also seem to provide no
special difficulty. My purpose in uttering that statement may
very well be to influence you to keep it, and part of the persuasive
power of my sentence may well derive from the emotive force
of the word 'ought'. Suppose, however, that I do not utter that
sentence out loud, but think to myself as I watch your behaviour

that you ought to keep the promise. Then I am making a silent judgement, which, being silent, cannot possibly influence your conduct. A supporter of the Emotive theory might say that what I am doing is mentally reminding myself always to have a feeling of approval towards promise-keeping, and to be sure that when I make a promise I keep it. If this is what I am really doing, then what demands explanation, and receives none, is why I should be so foolish as to cast *my* self-persuasion in the form of a sentence about what *you* ought to do. Similar difficulties arise with sentences such as "John ought to have kept his promise". These have to be interpreted as attempts to influence everyone within hearing to have an attitude of approval towards promise-keeping. But if that *is* what the sentence is used for, then would it not be clearer if we said so in a straightforward fashion instead of pretending that we were speaking about John. When we come to sentences such as "I ought to pay back the money I owe John Smith", the theory seems to lose any vestige of plausibility. If I utter the sentence to myself, so that no one hears it, then the only person I can be persuading is myself. The fact that I have already uttered the sentence means, on this theory, that I already have a feeling of moral approval towards paying back the money. If I don't now pay back the money but have to be further persuaded to do so, it does not seem likely that mere repetition of the statement will be a very effective means of persuasion.

There is a further problem about this persuasive version of the Emotive theory that we should look at. The fact that people do disagree and argue with one another about moral issues has always been a difficulty for purely subjectivist theories. For if I say that capital punishment is morally right and you say that it is not, then we seem to be disagreeing, and normally we would try to argue the matter out. Our argument would stop at once if we believed, as the subjectivist theory would have us believe, that our moral statements were nothing more than expressions of personal feeling. Now, the persuasive version of the Emotive theory claims to have met this difficulty and to leave room for argument. Our two sentences about capital punishment indicate a difference in our subjective attitude to it, and this is interpreted as a form of disagreement. The Emotive theorists claim that what we are trying to do in arguing with one another is to remove this difference in attitude. Part of our argument may consist in getting straightforward agreement about the facts of the situation. If agreement about the facts does not produce the same attitude, we may have to use exhortation and other forms of emotional persuasion. This, however, has the effect of turning a moral argument into a kind of propaganda. The difficulty here is obvious. In a serious moral argument there are limits to the kinds of persuasion one may legitimately use.

The Emotive theory, however, is not the only ethical theory that has been stimulated by the current philosophical preoccupation with problems of language and meaning. You will recall that statements like "Promise-keeping is right" were analysed into "I have an attitude of moral approval towards promise-keeping, pray do so as well". That last imperative clause was bound to attract attention. A number of philosophers became convinced that ethical language is essentially imperative in character. They claim that the function of moral utterances is to regulate or influence conduct, and one of the commonest ways in which conduct is regulated is by the utterance of commands. When a person says "You ought not to take that money" it is possible to convince oneself that this is another, possibly more polite, way of saying "Don't take that money". Now, it may very well be true that when we use moral language in the education of children our statements may have the force of commands. Indeed they may be intended to have the force of commands. It is not at all clear, however, that this is also true when two adults use the same language between themselves. There are two forms of language that may aim at influencing conduct. I may *request* you to close the door, or I may *command* you to close the door. Now, when we request someone to do something, we know that our request may or may not be acceded to, and this knowledge is part of the request use of language. A person may reply to our request to shut the door, by saying that he sees no reason why he should go to the trouble of closing the door; if we want it shut, then we can shut it ourselves. When we give a command, however, the situation is different in that we expect the command to be obeyed. Anyone may make a request, but not everyone can give a command and expect to have it obeyed. Commands are an appropriate form of utterance only when the person commanding and the person commanded stand in certain more or less clearly defined relations of authority. Where there is a recognized hierarchical command structure as in the army, it is wholly appropriate to give commands, not make requests, and to expect unquestioning obedience. The relations between parents and young children have something of this command structure. A parent may tell a child to do something and expect the child to obey. Most parents distinguish pretty clearly between those occasions on which they are exercising their parental prerogatives of command and those occasions when commanding or ordering are not appropriate. The average child also appears to be well able to distinguish those occasions. The difficulty in treating moral sentences as commands of any kind is that, outside the field of early moral education (and not everyone would agree that it is appropriate even there) there is nothing remotely resembling a command structure. If I were to say to someone "You ought to keep that promise to Mary", he might ask what I meant by saying he ought to. If I then replied "I am really telling you to keep it", the only appropriate response would be for him to say "Who do you think you are to give me orders" and to that I can see no reply that I can give—except to say that I wasn't ordering him at all, just trying out an ethical theory in which I don't really believe!

Although contemporary subjectivist theories were originally an offshoot of the positivist theory of meaning, they are now regarded as independent and grounded directly on the study of ethical language. But to try to account for what is involved in moral judgement by examining only certain functions of moral language doesn't seem to be satisfactory. A serious difficulty arises from the fact that many of the functions taken to be especially typical of moral sentences can be traced in many non-moral types of sentence. I have already pointed out how a simple statement about the existence of a subjective feeling, "I like ice-cream", can be used persuasively. To this we can add such statements as "Here is your coffee" when I hold out a cup, or "There's the door" said in a certain tone of voice. Both of these *can* be interpreted imperatively, although they look as if they were statements about the location of objects in space. Many contemporary theories about ethical language fail to distinguish between the function of a statement and its import, between the various reasons for which we may utter statements aloud and the literal meaning that these statements may have. The adherents of the Emotive and Imperativist theories of ethics have explored with great ingenuity many different functions of ethical language. Apparently they take it for granted that moral statements cannot possibly mean what they appear to mean. It may be extremely difficult to justify the claim that moral sentences do have a plain or literal meaning, in addition to their other functions. But simply to ignore the claim because it will not easily fit current linguistic preconceptions is surely equally difficult to justify.

In view of the manifest difficulties that face them, you may wonder how subjectivist theories were able to gain such popularity in the past quarter of a century. In all fairness I should say that a major reason why philosophers took them seriously was the very unconvincing accounts of the literal meaning of moral sentences given in the early part of this century. Broadly speaking, sentences of the type "Promise-keeping is right" were treated as analogous to such sentences as "Roses are red". Just as the roses are thought to have a property "redness" to which the word "red" refers, so actions like promise-keeping were thought to have what was called a non-natural property of "rightness". Non-natural properties cannot of course be observed by any of the senses, but it was alleged that they could be known by some kind of intellectual intuition. While we may sympathize with the subjectivists in their attempt to find a more convincing account of moral sentences than this, it is possible that a sounder interpretation of the way in which moral sentences have literal as well as emotive meaning might yet be produced. The belief that when we make a moral judgement we are doing something more than merely evincing our own feelings and endeavouring to influence the feelings and conduct of others may be a widespread illusion. But it is an extremely powerful illusion, which will be dispelled only by very much more powerful arguments than have so far been produced against it by subjectivists.

Let us look once again at the pure subjectivist form of the Emotive theory, which has had such a strong appeal in our century. The basic claim is that when I utter a moral sentence of the form "You ought to keep that promise" I am making no assertion but simply evincing my moral feeling. If two hours later I utter the sentence "You ought not to keep that promise" I am not, as you might think, contradicting myself. I am evincing another and different moral feeling in connection with the same thought of your keeping the promise. We cannot stop people changing their minds; but while there are some circumstances where no-one would seriously query the change of mind, there are others where we should expect to be given some justification of the change. If I say at eleven in the morning "I feel like going sailing tonight" and then at three in the afternoon I say "I don't feel like going sailing" I cannot be made to justify my change of mind or attitude towards sailing. Someone who had hoped to accompany me might peevishly ask why I had changed my mind, but I am entitled simply to say "I just don't feel like it anymore and that's that. There's no use arguing about it, and I didn't promise that I would go". Suppose now that I am speaking to John who had promised Susan that he would take her out sailing. I say at six o'clock "You ought to keep that promise" and then at seven o'clock "You ought not to keep that promise"; have we said all that there is to say about that situation when we have explained that all that has happened is that my moral feeling has changed? What seems to cry out for explanation is the widespread conviction that if it is a *moral* feeling that I am evincing in my remarks, then I must produce a convincing reason for my change of mind. If between six and seven John is called urgently to the hospital where his brother has been taken after a serious accident, I might well change my mind about his obligation to keep the promise to go sailing. The difficulty with the pure Emotive theory is that once we admit that moral feelings are attached to reasons, then moral sentences can no longer be regarded as the evincing of moral feeling *and nothing more*.

When we begin to inquire into the nature of the moral feeling, this difficulty seems to increase. When I say "You ought to keep your promise to go sailing" I almost certainly experience a moral feeling. But it would seem also that I am judging that your situation is such that you ought to keep the promise. And these two elements of feeling and judging seem inseparable. If called upon, I could give reasons for my moral judgement, just as I would for any other form of judgement. If it is all a matter of the having and not having of purely subjective feelings, then arguing and giving reasons seems utterly and totally out of place in connection with moral sentences. If we admitted that when a person utters a moral sentence, he is experiencing a moral feeling of some sort and also making a judgement that he can be called upon to defend with reasons, then we have abandoned pure subjectivism and we must turn to the task of explaining the sense in which the moral judgement can be regarded as objective.

Those who defend the Emotive theory have frequently said that there is no reason why adherents of the theory should begin to trample on their neighbours. Opponents of the theory have maintained that this precisely is the difficulty—there is no reason why they should or should not.

THE OBJECTIVITY OF MORAL JUDGEMENT 5

In my last talk we examined a number of purely subjectivist theories about the nature of moral judgement. None of them appeared to do justice to what we mean when we discuss a moral issue. Our next task must be to see whether we can say anything in favour of the view that moral judgements are objective; in other words, that they can be true or false like other judgements. From the point of view of ordinary moral practice, a firm belief in the objectivity of moral judgement is sufficient. But for a philosophical understanding of the nature of morality we must try to go beyond the mere belief in objectivity to the grounds that support it.

Let us begin then by asking how we should understand the antithesis between what is subjective and what is objective. These words began as technical terms in philosophy and then acquired a much wider currency. When we talk about a person having an experience, a simple one — like seeing an ash tray — that experience can be analysed into the subject who has the experience, who is doing the seeing, you or I, and the object that is being experienced or seen, the ashtray. On the one hand there is the mind of the person or subject and all that goes on within it, and on the other hand there is everything that exists in the world external to the mind. What goes on or exists in the external world can be experienced by more than one person; what goes on in the mind of a person is peculiar to that person, though it may be similar to what goes on in the mind of another. Both you and I can see the same ashtray, but you and I must each of us do our own seeing. What belongs to the common world may then be called objective and what happens in the mind of any person or subject may be called subjective. When I see the ashtray I may experience a feeling of dislike for it, whereas you, seeing the same ashtray, may experience a feeling of liking for it. The ashtray is objective, but our feelings are subjective. Although only I can experience my own feelings, they are just as real as your feelings and just as real as the ashtray. To say that anything is purely subjective certainly does not mean that it does not exist. Statements about what is subjective, however, may be harder to verify than statements about what is objective — harder, but not impossible. If you tell me that you like the ashtray, I may believe you or I may have grounds for thinking that you are insincere, that you don't in fact like it but are saying so in order to avoid hurting someone's feelings. In such circumstances it might still be possible for me to test the truth of your statement about your feelings by observing how you behave or listening to other things you say. If, for example, you let slip the further statement that you wouldn't buy one like it and wouldn't have it in your house, I would find it difficult to believe your assertion that you liked it.

Let us begin our explorations in this very sticky area by first considering what we might mean by denying that moral judgements are objective. That denial can take one form that we can dismiss fairly quickly. I mean the view that moral judgements never give expression to knowledge of any kind, but are all mere matters of opinion. Now, when anyone asserts that something is merely a matter of opinion, he usually does so because there is a good deal of difference among the various opinions that are being expressed. Often after a bout of argument, he will say "Well, that's simply your opinion about it. Mine's different". There does appear to be a good deal of disagreement about moral issues, and this probably lies behind the assertion that moral judgements are merely matters of opinion. However, if I hold an opinion about some matter, then it is a subjective fact about me that I hold the opinion. But in so far as it is an opinion *about* something, then it is either a true opinion about that something or it is false. And its truth or falsity will be determined, not by examining my subjective state, but by examining whatever it is that I am holding the opinion about. If moral judgements are indeed expressions of opinion, then they are either true or false — that is, they are objective — however hard it may be to determine the truth or falsity of any actual opinion. If the moral sentence "You ought to pay back that money" is not merely an expression of my feelings but expresses an opinion about what you ought to do, then it is either a true opinion or a false one. In order to determine which it is we should have to examine in detail the whole objective situation that led up to the judgement. Of course many people who have asserted that moral judgements are mere matters of opinion may really have meant to say that they are mere expressions of subjective feeling. But that is a different matter and we discussed the difficulties in that in my last talk.

You may object that this is not the real point at all in calling moral judgements mere opinions. The real trouble is that we can never be certain about moral judgements. Let us look at this claim. In the first place, what kind of moral judgements is the claim being made about? A man might feel quite certain about the truth of the general moral judgement that unjust or unfair action is wrong, and yet be very uncertain whether some act that he was about to do was really an example of unjust action. He could be certain about the general but uncertain about the particular moral judgement. Even if we admit this, it would not follow that moral judgements are not objective. Moreover, we can feel quite certain about *some* particular moral judgements. If I were to see a man deliberately torturing a small child I should be quite certain about the truth of the particular moral judgement that he was acting wrongly. Furthermore, uncertainty is not limited to moral judgements. When I state what I think is the correct answer to a complicated mathematical sum, I may feel far from certain that I am right, but we don't say that therefore mathematical judgements are not objective.

If we said that moral judgements are not objective simply because we feel uncertain about some of them, we should in consistency have to extend our denial to other types of judgement normally considered to be objective.

But can we even be certain about general moral judgements such as that torturing small children is wrong? This time we must ask what kind of certainty is meant. On the one hand there is what we may call absolute incontrovertible certainty. This is perhaps the kind of certainty people would like to have, but the plain fact is that this is possible only with regard to statements that are true by definition like "All bachelors are unmarried men". Of course we can be certain about that statement because the predicate is part of the meaning of the subject. Again, we can be certain about the statement "All murder is wrong" because murder means wrongful killing. The other kind of certainty is sometimes described as reasonable certainty. When a judge talks about what is beyond reasonable doubt, he recognizes that in practical affairs incontrovertible certainty is unattainable but reasonable certainty may be. This is the kind of certainty we reach when we have taken every possible precaution against error including consulting other people. Now, in this sense I have to confess that I am quite certain about the truth of the general moral judgement that torturing small children is wrong. If anyone differed from me on that point and suggested that as far as he could see it might be right, then not only is there a profound difference of opinion between us, but it is one in which I cannot possibly acquiesce. I should do everything in my power to prevent such a person securing a teaching or administrative post in an elementary school or any other institution in which small children are to be found, and I should regard it as my moral duty to do so. Here we meet an interesting feature of moral discussion. When the issue is a moral one, we cannot agree to differ as we may when it is a matter of taste. For centuries it has been said that you cannot argue about matters of taste, you must agree to differ. But when people differ on a moral issue, they will certainly argue about it and be seriously perturbed if they cannot agree. To attempt to break off a moral discussion by saying "There's no use arguing. We'll just have to agree to differ" is dangerously close to abandoning the moral point of view altogether. Disagreement about complicated moral issues may indeed cause us to feel uncertain about the truth of some moral judgements. However, we cannot make the fact that some moral judgements are uncertain a ground for saying that all are. Uncertainty by itself is not a sufficient ground for denying that moral judgements are objective.

There is another and tougher line of argument that we must consider. Moral judgements, as I have pointed out, are of different types, but the most important is that which asserts that some action ought to be done by someone. If it cannot be considered objective, then it is unlikely that any other kind will be. Now, you may say that I have not touched on the real reason why we cannot be certain about a judgement like "I ought to pay back the money I owe John Smith". This judgement only appears to imply that there is something about the objective situation that provides a ground for my judgement that I ought to pay back the money. In reality, however, you may say, the judgement does not rest on anything in the actual situation but is due to some kind of projection into my adult life of the kind of feeling that I used to have as a child when my parents were trying to teach me the moral rules. My strong feeling of obligation is perhaps nothing more than a kind of echo of the voice of authority that I was accustomed to as a child. In the modern jargon, I have been conditioned to feel like that about certain types of action. My so-called moral judgements are merely a reflection of this conditioning process, and do not have any objective basis in reality. Now this line of argument is fairly common today. It is a sophisticated form of moral subjectivism. What can we say about it?

In the first place, we must again make a distinction, a distinction between what I am going to call first-hand and second-hand moral judgements. By a second-hand moral judgement I mean all those moral sentences that we utter on appropriate occasions simply because we have been taught to do so and find the people around us doing so, the judgements that we make without thinking, the judgements for which we could produce no good reasons if we were challenged. Suppose that someone says that Jane did wrong in lifting some article from a shop without paying for it because theft is wrong. If he can produce no reason for thinking that theft is wrong except that he was taught so in his youth, then the judgement is an example of a second-hand moral judgement. It is probably a fairly safe generalization to suggest that the vast majority of moral beliefs and the judgements based on them are second hand in this sense. And these judgements may be accompanied by feelings that could well be explained psychologically along the lines I have outlined. Anyone drilled by constant repetition and threats of punishment into the belief that cheating is wrong may firmly believe that cheating is indeed wrong and when he thinks about cheating he may experience a strong feeling of revulsion against it. This is all fairly obvious and represents a phenomenon by no means confined to moral judgement. Many historical discussions among people who are not expert historians take place on the basis of nothing stronger or more reliable than historical beliefs inculcated during their schooldays, and such discussions may be coloured by feelings not much more mature than those experienced in the classroom. But neither historical nor moral judgements as such need be regarded as non-objective on these grounds. Only if first-hand moral judgements can be shown to have no objective grounds could we reasonably say that moral judgements lack objectivity.

To avoid possible misunderstanding, let me say that to call a moral judgement second hand in this sense does not mean that it is false. Quite a number of my beliefs about what happened in Canada two hundred years ago are second hand in the sense that I have accepted them on the authority of the historians whose books I have read. I did not reach them by considering all the evidence for myself. I believe that the historians are reliable and that the beliefs that I have accepted from them are true though second hand for me. It is to be hoped that the moral teaching given to children is also reasonably reliable. Moreover, it is quite impossible for anyone to convert all his second-hand beliefs into first-hand beliefs. By a first-hand belief of any kind, moral, historical, scientific, or what you will, I mean a belief that we hold because we have examined and weighed the evidence and could produce it if called upon to do so. The greater part of what we call our knowledge, historical and scientific, consists of second-hand beliefs, which we have accepted on authority, and provided that the authorities are reliable, there is no reason why this should not be so. It is clear, however, that the second-hand beliefs must rest on first-hand beliefs. While my own historical beliefs are for the most part second hand, I expect the professional historian to reach first-hand beliefs based on his detailed study of the historical evidence. I do not mean that professional historians will themselves have only first-hand beliefs. That would be too great a task for any man. But they must have at least some.

Before we look at what is involved in making an original moral judgement, there are still two preliminary points to note. In the first place, in the field of science and history first-hand judgements or beliefs can be achieved for the most part only by experts who have the time and training to examine and weigh the relevant evidence. The man in the street must look to the professional scientist or historian for guidance about what to believe. This is nòt so in the field of morality. The moral philosopher, whose task it is to think about morality and its implications, has no monopoly of first-hand judgements. Any intelligent person who has given any serious thought to morality and its problems may make an original moral judgement. Morality is not a matter for professionals but for everyman. Secondly, you may object that if I am right, making first-hand moral judgements must be a very rare occurrence. This may be so—I am not in a position to know, but I don't think it affects the argument. For all practical purposes, for the living of a good moral life, what matters is that we should have correct moral beliefs and act on them. It is when we are trying to reach a theoretical understanding of the nature of morality and what is involved in it that we must raise the question about the conditions under which a first-hand moral judgement may be made. I suggest that these conditions are most likely to be found in the kind of situation where a man is initially not sure what to do and must answer the question, what ought I to do?

Let us suppose then that I am in a situation where I must act but I don't at once see what it is that I ought to do. Perhaps I am not even sure what I want to do. But to ask "What do I want to do in this situation?" is quite different from asking "What ought

I to do?" and that is the question we are to discuss. Now, if the Emotive theory were correct, that is, if my moral judgement is merely the expression of feeling, then presumably I would have to sit back and wait until I was sure that I had a stronger feeling about one possible line of action than about any others. I could then express this by saying "I ought to do this". Then my moral judgement would be purely subjective. But surely it is a very odd procedure. It appears to me that in such a situation I don't try to examine what my feelings may happen to be (though there are occasions when this might be a relevant factor in my final decision), but rather I begin to think about the nature of the situation in which I find myself. The situation is not a part of me, as my feelings are. It is I who am part of the situation. In thinking about it, my attention is directed on something objective, which I am seeking to interpret in moral terms. But it is the situation as it really is that I am seeking to interpret. If the situation is one in which two of my moral beliefs come into conflict, then, whatever I do, I cannot simply utter a second-hand moral belief of the type I have described. Let us suppose that there are only two alternatives open to me, which we will call action X and action Y. If I do action X, then I shall be involved in telling a very serious lie; and if I do action Y, I shall be involved in breaking a solemn promise that I made to an old friend who is trusting me. I am unwilling to tell a lie, which I regard as wrong, and I am unwilling to break my promise, which I also consider to be morally wrong. I have, let us say, never before thought about why lying or breaking promises is wrong. I have simply accepted the belief that they are wrong from the days of my early moral education. If I am to make a genuine moral judgement about what I ought to do in this situation, then I must examine the grounds on which these beliefs are based. In the course of doing this, I discover that there are good reasons for both. Neither can be abandoned lightly. I must also consider the possible consequences of doing X and of doing Y. Knowing that I have a distinct inclination to do Y, I must take steps to be sure that my analysis of the situation and my judgement are not being biased by this desire to do Y. It is always easy to find specious reasons for doing what one wants to do, but the task before me is that of discovering what I *ought* to do. Eventually, after I have examined the grounds of my beliefs and the various factors in the situation, I must make a judgement that, let us say, X is what I ought to do. I may in these circumstances feel uncertain about my judgement, and say to a friend "I think that X is what I ought to do, but I could be wrong". There is nothing at all odd in a remark like that. A classical scholar seeking for the correct reading in an obscure text may say "I think the correct reading is such and such, but I could be wrong". Now, this judgement that I make about what I ought to do does not appear to be a mere expression of some feeling that I happen to be experiencing. I am aware that someone may disagree with my judgement and in the course of discussion I might even be brought to change my mind. But when I make it, it has all the marks of a judgement about an objective situation, which could, if necessary, be defended by producing reasons for it.

I don't want to suggest that this lengthy process of thought either does or should happen every time that we make a moral judgement. The tempo of life does not permit such extensive examination of all moral situations. My point rather is that this kind of situation may jolt us into a degree of serious thought never before directed upon our moral beliefs, and the judgement that results will be grounded upon reasons that may be laid out for inspection by other people. Since in a moral situation we are not dealing with the abstractions of pure mathematics, but with the living complexity of the real world in which we have to act, we certainly cannot expect that our moral judgement will appear as something incontrovertibly demonstrated. In much the same way that we interpret the events in nature as taking place in space and time, so we interpret the realm of human action in terms of right and wrong, good and bad. Since we are fallible human beings, any actual judgement may be wrong, just as the judgement of a scientist may be wrong on occasion—as, for example, Rutherford's judgement that atomic power would not be available for human use in this century. In so far as the judgement can be supported by reasons that can be scrutinized by other people and is not merely about my state of mind but about the objective moral situation itself, the moral judgement has all the objectivity that is necessary.

The word 'objectivity' has been so loosely used in recent times that there has been a tendency to equate objectivity with truth, which is absurd. An objective account of any kind may turn out to be false; its objectivity rests in the fact that it can be shown to be false. In terms of the account of what is objective and what is subjective that I gave at the beginning of this talk, the moral judgement falls on the side of the objective.

It is obvious that if in my analysis of the situation I make a mistake about the facts, then I am more than likely to reach an erroneous judgement about what ought to be done. A great many instances of moral disagreement rest upon different beliefs about the nature of the facts, and when agreement about the facts can be secured, moral agreement usually follows. A great many of the moral differences between different social groups can be explained along these lines. The Chuckchee son who regards it as his moral duty to kill his aging father does so because he holds the factual belief that a man will continue for ever in the state in which he is at death. Therefore, it is in his father's best interests that he be killed while still vigorous and vital. His to us quite abhorrent moral belief rests on what to us is a thoroughly mistaken view of the facts about human life and survival. How far would moral differences disappear if people agreed about the facts? We could find this out by empirical investigation. But this demands long and patient work. Moral disagreement can be regarded as just as much of an intellectual challenge as scientific disagreement between two theories about the nature of light.

At this point you may object that in scientific argument it is always possible to settle the matter by recognized methods of procedure, and these are lacking in the field of morality. To answer this objection in full would demand an extremely detailed examination of the methods and assumptions of both natural science and moral philosophy, which we cannot possibly enter into here. There are some points, however, which I should make in this connection. In the first place, we must not exaggerate the extent to which science presents a monolithic facade of universally accepted beliefs. Disagreement on scientific matters is far from unknown, and a scientific controversy may be settled only after very lengthy inquiries. Some disagreement on even major ethical issues is to be expected and history shows that some ethical controversies have been settled. I should hardly expect anyone today seriously to defend the view that slave-owning is right and slavery a morally justifiable institution, and yet there was disagreement about that not a hundred years ago. Secondly, science is not built up through the purely individual efforts of a series of isolated persons. Science is a co-operative activity and part of scientific method is the submission of findings and theories to the judgement of other scientists. This is not incompatible with the fact that individual scientists have constantly to exercise their own judgement. Similarly in morality, each person has constantly to exercise his own judgement, but there is a method of dealing with disputes even if it is hard to apply, namely joint discussion, which has the double aim of trying to make sure that the disputants have got the facts right and of trying to counteract the pressures of subjective influence in the form of personal desires and emotions. A perfectly legitimate question in a moral discussion may take the form "Are you sure you are not being unduly influenced by such and such an emotion or desire?". If a person is not prepared to face a question of that order, then he is not genuinely taking part in a moral discussion.

It is perhaps worth emphasizing this point. We know a good deal about the sort of influences that lead to distorted thinking in the field of moral discussion. An article in a popular magazine described the results obtained in a questionnaire about how people would judge morally in a series of very different situations. It was found that there was little disagreement about fundamental moral principles but considerable disagreement about their interpretation in individual cases. Some people were prepared to justify acts of petty shoplifting on the grounds that this was simply a method of squaring accounts with large stores that practise systematic deception on the public through exaggerated advertising claims. The same people were also quite convinced that stealing is wrong. This, however, is surely specious argument by any standard. It was also found that where a person's interests were unfavourably affected by the action of someone else, that action was judged by the strictest moral standards; if the same action favourably affected a person's interests, then that action was quite differently interpreted. Since human actions do tend to affect the welfare of other people it is not surprising that the judgements passed on them should sometimes be biased by the pressure of subjective factors. However, only if all moral judgements, even those subjected to the most stringent forms of criticism, are inevitably biased by subjective factors would we be forced to conclude that the moral judgement has an indelible taint of subjectivity. There is no incontrovertible evidence that would demonstrate this to be the case. Like all judgements, the moral judgement is subject to distorting influences — but, as in other judgements, these can be counteracted.

To avoid a possible misunderstanding, let me say in conclusion that the view that moral judgements are objective does not entail a belief in absolute moral standards attained by any actual, historical social group. There is only one standard that could be regarded as in any reasonable sense absolute, and that is attainable by any person at any time and in any social group. I refer to the standard represented by the endeavour to do only those actions that, after due reflection, the individual has come to believe are right. No man can be expected to achieve any higher standard and it is open to every man to achieve at least that.

RELIGION AND MORALITY

6

Religion and morality exist together in nearly all societies we know of, and tend to be easily confused with one another. Many writers have simply assumed that morality always has a religious foundation, an assumption which does not appear to be warranted by the evidence. On the other hand, there are religions — among which Christianity is perhaps the most notable — that do try to inculcate among their adherents a characteristic moral outlook. However, it is not my intention in this talk to discuss the specifically moral teaching attached to any religion. What I want to do is to talk about the way in which moral experience has been invested with tremendous significance by certain aspects of religious teaching. Whatever else it involves, a religion will include at least some beliefs about the general nature of the universe. In the Western, Christian tradition for example, one central belief is that the universe is governed by a divine being. And it is with problems that have arisen within this tradition that I shall be concerned.

In my talks so far I have suggested that in discussing morality we are chiefly concerned with the experience of moral obligation, with beliefs that there are certain types of actions that we ought to do and others that we ought not to do. These beliefs, as we have seen, are frequently expressed in the form of moral rules of conduct. Although rules of conduct form part of the essence of morality, we also saw that the ground of these rules must be looked for in something beyond the rules themselves, in some idea of a common good or in the goodness of some pattern or way of life. It is when we begin to ask questions about the nature of this common good or this way of life and its relation to the individual that we begin to meet the really difficult problems raised by morality. And it is at this point that religious issues begin to impinge upon our discussion, and they cannot to be ignored if we are to do justice to the subject. To suggest that some way of life is peculiarly appropriate to man is to touch upon these fundamental problems about the nature and destiny of man, which historically have occupied so much of the attention both of the great religions of the world and of the great philosophers of the past. In talking about these problems we are certainly entering upon a highly speculative area, but for reasons that I will try to make plain, we cannot afford wholly to neglect these speculations.

Let us begin by asking whether it is possible for morality to exist without religion. On the face of it the answer to that question might appear to be a simple "Yes, of course". If we are to have an ordered society in which everyone has a reasonable chance to live in peaceful enjoyment of all the good things of life, then we must all be prepared to observe certain basic ground rules of conduct, the so-called moral rules. In any group of human beings there are bound to be competing interests, and to avoid the dominance of all by the few who are strong and unscrupulous, there must be general agreement that we shall all observe these rules. To put the matter in this way, however, at once forces us to pose the question "What do we do about those members of society who simply will not obey the rules that the rest of us are prepared to observe, or who do not see why they should follow the rules when it would apparently be to their advantage to break them?". We cannot run a country without some form of taxation. Reasonable people recognize that fact, and pay their taxes. There are people, however, who seek to avoid payment of their taxes either from sheer selfishness or from complete failure to appreciate the conditions of organized political existence. We deal with these people by punishing them if they are caught. To use the language that was popular in the nineteenth century, we apply sanctions to them.

Now, moral philosophers have generally divided sanctions into three groups known as the legal, the religious, and the social sanctions. The legal sanctions are largely the penalties attached to the violation of duly promulgated laws. The religious sanctions are the penalties and rewards that it is believed the divine being attaches to the violation of or obedience to His commands. The social sanctions are the various pressures that members of society can bring to bear upon us to ensure that we do not stray too far from what is generally considered to be the right and proper path of conduct. It has been said that sanctions are nothing but a means of making or forcing a person to act as if he were a good and upright person even when he is not. The thought behind this jibe is of course that the kind of person we should be prepared to call genuinely good and upright is precisely the person who will act rightly without suffering external pressure from other persons, who will act rightly because this seems to him to be the reasonable thing to do:

In our moments of moral strength we may feel no need for such sanctions, but in our moments of moral weakness — and what human being does not experience such moments? — in our moments of weakness the thought of sanctions may be all that is needed to help us to resist the temptation to put mere self-interest before what we know we ought to do. And here we meet the real problem. As long as life is proceeding reasonably smoothly, making no greater demands on us than we can fairly easily shoulder, we are unlikely to experience any really serious clash between our moral obligations and what we conceive to be our self-interest. The thought of sanctions is then virtually irrelevant. However, in my first talk I mentioned the newspaper report about twenty people in Toronto who indicated that they were prepared to break nearly every rule in our moral code if they thought they could remain undetected. That is, if they lived in a world in which there were no external pressures to conform with the rules, no sanctions of the type I have mentioned, then they would pay no attention to the rules but simply do what they happened to feel like doing. It is reasonable to suppose that in so far as our twenty moral rebels do in fact toe the moral line, they do so simply because they are afraid that they might be caught. Put in its crudest form, the question we are now approaching is this: When conformity to the accepted moral rules of society doesn't fairly obviously result in some advantage to ourselves, why should we bother to conform to these rules? And the crudest answer that can be given to that question is to say that if you don't conform to the rules sanctions will be applied against you. Quite bluntly, you will be punished if you are caught, and that may be expected to be unpleasant. This is a very ancient answer to the question, and it was already bitterly criticized by Plato over two thousand years ago. Crude though it is, this answer has survived in some of the accounts that have been offered of the relation between religion and morality.

According to one religious view the laws of morality are identified with the laws of God. Failure to obey the laws of God will be visited by severe punishment, if not in this life then in the pains of hell to be experienced in an afterlife. Faithful obedience to the laws of God on the other hand will result in the enjoyment of rewards, if not in this life, then in some heavenly afterlife. As an answer to our problem of how to deal with the conflict between duty and self-interest in the life of the individual the doctrine of divine sanctions is satisfactory neither to religion nor to morality. On the one hand, it can degenerate very easily into a wretched caricature of true religion by reducing it to a kind of long-term fire insurance. According to this conception the religious man would never face a genuine conflict between moral obligation and self-interest. He would merely have to choose between short-term and long-term self-interest. It is difficult to imagine how there could be grafted onto this view any belief in a genuinely personal relationship between a believer and his God. Moreover, this view would go no way towards satisfying the demands of any developed form of morality. Although morality may begin with the demand that our outward conduct should conform with the rules, in its higher forms morality has set far higher ideals before men. Our inner motives are also expected to reflect the spirit of morality and the highest moral motive is often described as the desire to do what is right because that is the reasonable thing to do. A developed moral being realizes that he is not merely a separate individual but an integral part of a community of persons. We become persons only through our relations with other persons, and it is from this fact that our mutual obligations arise. Moral philosophers have sometimes expressed this by saying that the type of sanctions I have mentioned so far are all external. The truly moral sanction is to be found in our rational understanding of the conditions under which personal life is possible.

I should like now to illustrate some aspects of this difficult problem of the relation between religion and morality by comparing the views of two outstanding moral philosophers, the eighteenth-century German idealist, Immanuel Kant, and the nineteenth-century Utilitarian, Henry Sidgwick.

Sidgwick's impressive book *The Methods of Ethics* was once described as "on the whole the best treatise on moral theory that has ever been written". In this book Sidgwick defended with great skill and ingenuity the view that it is right and reasonable that we human beings should do what we believe will ultimately lead to the universal Good, which he identified with happiness. In the end the reason why we have moral rules of conduct is that if we obey them then we shall achieve a state of society in which it will be possible for the greatest number of persons to enjoy the greatest amount of happiness. There can be no doubt that many people will feel sympathetic towards this account. However, towards the end of this argument Sidgwick claims that it is essential that we should be able to prove or postulate a connection between virtue and self-interest if we are to avoid ultimate and fundamental contradiction in our ideas of what is reasonable in conduct. This is significant; for Sidgwick maintains that he can find no adequate grounds for believing that those who do what is right will be adequately rewarded and that those who do wrong will be punished. He argues that if we could believe in the existence of a just and benevolent God, then a connection between virtue and self-interest might well be established. Divine sanctions, he claims, would suffice to make it always in everyone's interests to promote universal happiness to the best of his knowledge. He does not believe that if we fail to establish a connection between duty and self-interest we should have to abandon morality altogether. In most cases, both our self-interest and our natural sympathy for our fellow human beings would still lead us to act rightly and reasonably towards them. But, he argues, in the cases where duty comes into conflict with self-interest, then reason would be divided against itself and could not be a motive on either side. The issue would have to be decided between two groups of non-rational impulses, and this presumably, since reason has abdicated, would be a matter of sheer chance. Here in Sidgwick we have the example of a great and profound humanist who apparently can conceive of a connection between religion and morality only in terms of divine sanctions, precisely the point of view that I have suggested is satisfactory neither to morality nor religion.

Immanuel Kant, on the other hand, famous as the austere moralist of duty, was determined to vindicate the independence of morality from all religious sanctions. "Morality" he wrote on one occasion "in no way needs religion for its support . . . but by means of pure practical reason is sufficient to itself." In his analysis of moral action, of what is involved in fulfilling our moral obligations, he attempted to show that universal reason by itself is capable of providing a motive to right action that transcends all thought of self-interest. Kant saw man as a creature compounded of reason and natural appetite. What he called the dignity of man rests on the fact that man is capable of rising above mere appetite and acting according to the dictates of pure reason. This is indeed a lofty conception of human nature, very far removed from the view of human nature that is current in our own day, and which is illustrated in much contemporary literature. In Norman Mailer's novel *The Naked and the Dead*, one of the characters is made to say "Freud's idea is that man is a worthless bastard and the only problem is how best to control him". Whether this is a correct interpretation of Freudian teaching is not to the point. It is how the public, with perhaps more insight than it is given credit for, sees the implications of his teaching.

While Sidgwick seemed to think that religion may be needed

in order to give morality a helping hand, Kant thought that morality was able to lend a helping hand to religion. It was Kant who originated the moral argument for the existence of God. According to Kant, the existence of moral obligation implies that there is an objective moral order in the universe. To secure the just distribution of happiness according to desert it is necessary, he claimed, to postulate the existence of a just God who will look after the morally deserving. I should emphasize that for Kant the right to happiness must first be morally earned and is not something we are born with. Kant's argument has been rightly criticized as having two obvious defects from the religious point of view. In the first place, as a critic once rather unkindly expressed it, all that his argument could be regarded as proving would be the existence of a kind of Divine Paymaster. We human beings do our moral work and at the Divine Pay Table we receive our just wages. What the argument again does not show is that there exists a personal God who could inspire devotion in his worshippers. Secondly, the argument does not really require that there should be a separate divine being at all. It would be sufficient for his purposes if we could regard the universe as exhibiting a fundamental moral order, which would not offend even a confirmed atheist.

It does not seem to me that either of these attempts to bring morality into relation with religion can be regarded as satisfactory. The Utilitarian humanist sees religion as possibly providing a powerful motive to right conduct through the conception of divine sanctions. The Kantian humanist sees morality as completely independent or autonomous, and consequently has no real place for religion at all. Although both Kant and Sidgwick belong to the tradition of Western, Christian civilization neither of them can be regarded as essentially religious thinkers. If we now turn to philosophers with a definite religious cast of mind, we are given a very different account of the relation between religion and morality. Specifically Christian thinkers claim that the supreme Christian contribution is the revelation that God is not an utterly transcendent being, residing, like the Gods of the Greek philosopher Epicurus, in distant regions of infinite space and supremely indifferent to the fate of man. In the Christian tradition, God is represented as a being who cares for His creatures; His nature is described as constituted of love. Correlative to this conception of the nature of God are the two supreme commands given to His people that they shall love God with all their heart and all their strength and their neighbours as themselves. If you start from this conception of the nature of the relation between God and humanity —and it is difficult to see from what other point Christian thinkers could start—the relation between religion and morality must be very different from that suggested by Sidgwick or postulated by Kant. If we view morality as essentially concerned with the ways in which human beings ought to conduct themselves towards one another, then it would seem that when religion impinges on morality it must be conceived as providing both a unique motive for moral conduct and a general conception of human nature in terms of which human life can be lived. The supreme motive to moral conduct for the Christian is that of love for his fellow human beings and through this he expresses his love for God. And if the accepted Christian account of the nature of love is correct, then this would lift morality right out of the sphere of rewards and punishments. The Christian conception of human nature is as far removed from Freud's worthless bastard as it is possible to be; for the Christian conceives man as the child of God and therefore as of infinite worth.

Let us now go back to the question from which this discussion started: Can morality exist without religion? We can now see that the question was really ambiguous. If by morality we mean simply the beliefs that people hold to the effect that there are actions that ought to be done and others that ought not to be done—and this is the first meaning we distinguished—then the answer is surely that morality can exist without religion. An atheist with no sympathy for religion at all is still a member of society and can recognize the necessity for rules of conduct and the distinction between right and wrong. On the other hand, if we take morality in the second sense that we distinguished, as meaning not only our beliefs about right and wrong but also the extent to which and the way in which people live up to their beliefs, then the answer must be different. It will depend on our general interpretation of the kind of universe we live in. As I pointed out, religion always involves some general beliefs about the nature of the universe, and it is at this point that the connection will appear.

The Utilitarian humanist like Sidgwick, whose standards for human conduct were very high indeed, is haunted by a deep-rooted doubt whether men are capable of putting their moral duty towards their fellow men before their self-interest. To resolve his doubt he needs a divinely governed universe. The moralistic humanist like Kant, whose conception of the moral potentialities of human nature is lofty in the extreme, asserts that morality has no need of religion but can rest on the power of reason alone. Kant said that two things filled him with never ending awe: the starry heavens above and the moral law within; the order of the physical universe as revealed by science and man's capacity to rise above his animal nature and act as a free and rational being. It is significant of Kant's deep-rooted humanism that the thought of a creative and loving God was not among the things that filled him with awe. The Christian believer, on the other hand, while admitting the possibility of a humanist morality, holds that that morality reaches its highest point of achievement when it is transformed from within by the Christian conception of love for God and for one's fellow men.

At this point we seem to have moved very far away from the type of problems I was concerned with in my earlier talks. We started from an analysis of fairly mundane matters: What is the nature of a moral judgement, how many types are there, and what kind of arguments can be advanced to support them? Now we appear to be standing on the edge of vast metaphysical speculations concerning the very constitution of the universe. What has happened is that we have been led to consider the sort of impact that the demands of morality may make upon the life of the individual. It is really an old and familiar theme — the clash between the stern, hard call of duty and the tempting lure of immediate self-interest. Here it seems to me that we must raise two very fundamental problems. What comfort can be offered to the man who decides, in full awareness of what he is doing, to follow the call of duty even at the cost of considerable sacrifice of his apparent self-interest, even perhaps at the risk of death? The Roman Regulus returned to Carthage rather than break his oath, knowing that it meant death. We do well to remember that many men have in the past taken their morality with the utmost seriousness. We may wonder whether such men have to be assured that in the end it will all be made up to them or whether it is possible for a human being on occasion to act in a manner that transcends all thought of mere self-interest. If we claim that history contains numerous examples of men who have placed the claims of duty before those of self-interest, the sceptic will question our interpretation of human nature. And this leads me to my second question. What does the fact of moral obligation imply about the nature of man? Or, to put the question in a slightly different way, can the moral philosopher claim to have completed his task of interpreting moral experience if he does not go on to offer some account of human nature — unless he make some attempt to answer the question "What is man?"? Kant once remarked that this question summarizes all the questions of philosophy. If he is right, then we seem to have reached the point of saying that in order to do justice to all that is involved in moral experience we should have to range through the whole length and breadth of philosophy.

If we were to glance at the history of philosophy we should find that until quite recent times the major moral philosophers did not hesitate to embark on the troublesome seas of metaphysical speculation in their endeavours to reach an adequate interpretation of moral experience. The twentieth century, however, has witnessed one of the most powerful anti-metaphysical movements in the history of Western philosophy, and in consequence many contemporary philosophers have limited themselves to the logical analysis of moral concepts. Problems about the nature and destiny of man are nowadays pronounced to be insoluble in principle and quite unfit to occupy the attention of serious philosophers. The final question that I want to raise and leave with you is this: Can we really accept the embargo that some contemporary philosophers have attempted to lay upon all metaphysical discussion?

Obviously I cannot attempt to discuss such a far reaching question in my last few minutes, but I should like to conclude my talks by offering a suggestion for your consideration. It seems to me that after following the well-worn path of the logical analysis of moral concepts, the moral philosopher comes to a fork in the road. He must either decide that he can go no further or he must be prepared to venture along one of the two paths that lie ahead. The one path leads to what is often called a purely naturalistic interpretation of human nature. Man, on this view, is nothing more than the most highly organized creature in the animal kingdom, the most recent product of a blind process of evolution. This view has two great advantages. It clearly fits most neatly into the contemporary preoccupation with natural science and the various philosophies that have been founded on it. More important still, it can be clearly and intelligibly stated in the clean-cut, unambiguous language that science has forged for itself. If this view is taken seriously, then it must be recognized that human life is indeed "a tale told by an idiot, full of sound and fury, signifying nothing". The more hard-headed naturalistic thinkers have accepted this, but the more sentimentally minded have twisted themselves into logical knots in the endeavour to avoid it and retain a belief in morality.

The other path leads to what has been called a spiritual interpretation of human nature. On this view, man is indeed still an animal in the sense that he has an animal body, but he is considered capable in his moral conduct of bearing witness to something in himself that is other than and more than merely animal. This view has no such obvious advantages as the naturalistic view, and above all it suffers from the lack of any simple and straightforward language in which to express itself. Human attempts to state in language the nature of the spiritual have up to now always suffered from defects of vagueness and variability. There has none the less been an impressive number of attempts to overcome this problem. It was a religious writer who gave concise poetic expression to the difficulties of this view when he wrote "for now we see through a glass, darkly".

Yes, you may now say, we know that in the past there have been great naturalistic and great spiritual systems of thought, but this is the twentieth century, the century of science, and we cannot be expected to take this sort of thing seriously any more. The moral philosopher, if he is wise, will stop at the fork in the road and claim that he can go no further than logical analysis will take him. On this I would make two observations. The purely naturalistic interpretation of man does indeed belong to the past. It has perhaps never been more powerfully stated than by the Roman philosopher-poet Lucretius some two thousand years ago. The mistake would be to imagine that the fork in the road has never been visible before. And secondly, the moral philosopher has never in the past gone further than logical analysis will take him—nor is he now asked to do so. Only he must not stop before his task of analysis is complete. I have been suggesting that on occasion our moral experience seems to set before us a hard choice between duty and self-interest; whatever our choice may be, whether it be to follow duty or to seek our own interest, it represents what on our part can only be called an act of faith. There remains the task of analysing all that is involved in that act of faith. That used to be called metaphysics. In the twentieth century it might be better to call it something else. Whatever it is called, it does seem to be a task laid upon the moral philosopher. In the twentieth century the refusal to undertake this task represents the line of easy conformity. It is only the more adventurous minded who will continue to strive and wrestle with the difficulties of language in the hope of doing justice to the protesting spirit of man.

BIBLIOGRAPHY

INTRODUCTORY WORKS

Carritt, E. F., *Theory of Morals*, Oxford University Press, 1928.

Field, G. C., *Moral Theory*, Methuen, London, 1935.

Frankena, W. K., *Ethics*, Prentice Hall, New York, 1963.

SOME HISTORICAL CLASSICS

Plato (*c.* 427-347 B.C.), *The Republic, Protagoras and Meno,* and *Gorgias*, Penguin Classics (L48, L68, & L94), Penguin Books, Harmondsworth.

Aristotle (384-322 B.C.), *Nichomachean Ethics*, The World's Classics (546), Oxford University Press.

Selby-Bigge, L. A. (ed.), *British Moralists* (selections — mainly eighteenth century), The Library of Liberal Arts (152), Bobbs-Merrill, New York.

Kant, Immanuel (1724-1804), *Fundamental Principles of the Metaphysic of Morals* (1785), The Library of Liberal Arts (16), Bobbs-Merrill, New York.

Mill, J. S. (1806-73), *Utilitarianism* (1861), The Library of Liberal Arts (1), Bobbs-Merrill, New York.

Sidgwick, H. (1838-1900), *The Methods of Ethics* (1874), Papermac (19), Macmillan, London.

Bradley, F. H. (1846-1924), *Ethical Studies* (1876), Oxford Paperbacks (39), Oxford University Press.

SOME TWENTIETH-CENTURY CONTRIBUTIONS

Moore, G. E., *Principia Ethica*, Cambridge University Press, 1903, (paperback).

Ross, W. D., *The Right and the Good*, Clarendon Press, Oxford, 1930.

Leon, P., *The Ethics of Power*, Allen and Unwin, London, 1935.

Reid, L. A., *Creative Morality*, Allen and Unwin, London, 1936.

Stevenson, C. L., *Ethics and Language*, Yale Paperback (Y19), Yale University Press, 1944.

Ewing, A. C., *The Definition of Good*, Macmillan, London, 1947.

Plamenatz, J., *The English Utilitarians*, Blackwell, Oxford, 1949.

Prichard, H. A., *Moral Obligation*, Clarendon Press, Oxford, 1949.

Toulmin, S., *The Place of Reason in Ethics*, Cambridge University Press, 1950, (paperback).

Macbeath, A., *Experiments in Living*, Macmillan, London, 1952.

Hare, R. M., *The Language of Morals*, Oxford Paperbacks (77), Oxford University Press, 1952.

Nowell-Smith, P. H., *Ethics*, Pelican Book (A293), Penguin Books, Harmondsworth, 1954.

Mayo, B., *Ethics and the Moral Life*, Macmillan, London, 1958.

Maclagan, W. G., *The Theological Frontiers of Ethics*, Allen and Unwin, London, 1961.

Aiken, H. D., *Reason and Conduct*, Knopf, New York, 1962.

MORAL PHILOSOPHY